STRETCHED

Praise for *Stretched: A Study for Lent & the Entire Christian Life*

"The Christian life is one long Lent as we are given daily to die to sin and rise to walk in the newness of life. To paraphrase Luther, the Christian is a perpetual penitent. In this engaging book, Pastor Christopher Richmann helps us appreciate Lent not merely as a liturgical relic but as an ongoing exercise of repentance and faith. He shows readers from the Scriptures, that the Christian life begins in death but is stretched toward the resurrection of our bodies because Christ Jesus died for us and is risen for our justification. Suitable for individual meditation as well as a group study, *Stretched* invites us to take a deeper look at Lent and its disciplines through the lens of the theology of the cross."

—John T. Pless,
Concordia Theological Seminary, Fort Wayne, Indiana

"Christopher Richmann's study of Lent is informative, thought-provoking and challenging. Its emphases reach deep into Lent and beyond. Richmann has a knack for connecting historic Christian themes to issues in American Christianity and the broader American context today, addressing these deftly and cogently. Use it for a Lenten study in your congregation or use it for your own personal study. You will be both unsettled and consoled."

—Mary Jane Haemig,
Professor *emerita*, Luther Seminary, St. Paul, MN

"The season of Lent can be tricky, with many religious practices and often much religious posturing! Christopher Richmann has written a great guide to Lent for everyday Christians, interesting and engaging, written to provide a pathway through this season. This would be a wonderful book for small groups and circles, as well as individuals and church book clubs. I highly recommend it!"

—Mark Granquist,
Luther Seminary, St. Paul, Minnesota

"In an era of narcissistic cotton candy spirituality, Richmann draws out the robust dimensions of Lent, the season of the church year devoted to baptismal discipleship, to help us discern that the entire scope of the Christian life is one that draws us to daily repentance, increasingly conforming us to the crucified Christ. If you find yourself broken by the platitudes and false promises of contemporary Evangelicalism, and hunger for a truthful approach to the Christian faith, this is a must-read book."

—Mark Mattes,
Lutheran Bible Institute Chair of Theology,
Grand View University, Des Moines, Iowa

"Those who give up chocolate for Lent are liable to miss the point, but this fine book does not. Grounded in Scripture, Luther's insights, and pastoral experience, Richmann boldly proclaims that God himself chooses to subject his children to the trials of true "Lenten disciplines" through all of life, thereby creating strong faith and conforming them—you!—to Jesus. A rich, engaging, and bracing resource for group and personal use."

—Andrew Ronnevik,
Lecturer in Theology, Martin Luther Seminary,
Papua New Guinea

STRETCHED

A Study For Lent & The Entire Christian Life

FOREWORD BY Steven D. Paulson

CHRISTOPHER J. RICHMANN

FIFTEEN-SEVENTEEN PUBLISHING
1517.

Published by:
1517 Publishing
PO Box 54032
Irvine, CA 92619-4032

Publisher's Cataloging-in-Publication
(Provided by Cassidy Cataloguing Services, Inc.)

Names: Richmann, Christopher J., author. | Paulson, Steven D., writer of foreword.
Title: Stretched : a study for Lent and the entire Christian life / Christopher J. Richmann ; foreword by Steven D. Paulson.
Description: Irvine, CA : 1517 Publishing, [2026] | Includes bibliographical references.
Identifiers: ISBN: 9781964419381 (paperback) | 9781964419398 (ebook)
Subjects: LCSH: Lent—Biblical teaching. | Christian life. | God (Christianity)—Omnipotence. | Death—Religious aspects—Christianity. | Fasting—Religious aspects—Christianity. | Temptation. | Repentance—Christianity. | Piety. | BISAC: RELIGION / Holidays / Easter & Lent. | RELIGION / Biblical Studies / Bible Study Guides. | RELIGION / Christian Living / Spiritual Growth.
Classification: LCC: BV85 .R53 2026 | DCC: 242.34—dc23

Printed in the United States of America.
Cover art by Zachariah James Stuef.

Table of Contents

Foreword

THEOLOGY IS FOR PEOPLE in trouble. The specific theology of this book, known as "theology of the cross," is typically reserved for the most significant troubles. Nevertheless, though it is the most important word anyone could receive, the cross is often received last. Preachers even have a saying about this: When a man is in trouble, he first goes to his lawyer. When that doesn't work, he makes an appointment with his doctor. When that fails, he calls the undertaker. Only when he's in the ground does he think, "It's time to call the preacher." Your most significant trouble in life—anyone's life— is death, and its only treatment is the resurrection of the gospel. Along the way, we preachers are happy to deal with your sin, and even fend off the attacks of the Devil, but our superpower is in the word of Christ that unbinds death and raises you from the tomb.

Paul wrote best about this in responding to the questions of his Corinthian church concerning the resurrection of the body. First, you need to know about Christ's resurrection: "For I delivered to you as of first importance what I also received: that Christ died for your sins in accordance with the Scriptures, that he was buried, that he was raised on the third day in accordance with the Scriptures" (1 Cor 15:3-4). We call this "the creed" that we repeat whenever we get together with other Christians. Then Paul says, "Now, if Christ is proclaimed as raised from the dead, how can some of you say that there is no resurrection of the dead?" (1 Cor 15:12). You are going against the facts! You are denying the obvious! You are denying death and know nothing about life! In this regard, Pastor Richmann discusses the work of psychiatrist Ernest Becker, a favorite Jewish truth-teller in his book, *The Denial of Death*. People will go to any lengths—even to kill themselves—rather than admit the truth of death and resurrection for Christ and themselves.

Paul subsequently stops for a moment, overwhelmed by shame and disbelief that his parish at Corinth has fallen prey to the delusion that death is not real and that resurrection is an unnecessary fraud. He reminded them that "in Adam—all die" (1 Cor 15:22a). They are not originally "good creations" but are, instead, originally born in sin. Yet, in Christ—the new Adam—"all shall be made alive" (1 Cor 15:22b). Of course, this happened to Christ first (the "first fruits"), who took on their sin and died as a result. Then, "each in his own order...finally comes the End" (1 Cor 15:24). What happens in the End? Where are we all going? What is Christ doing after he is raised from the dead? Christ reigns! He then puts all enemies under his feet (1 Cor 15:25), and the very "last enemy to be destroyed is death" (1 Cor 15:26).

Okay, Paul, that sounds monumental, but then, why has Christ left us alone down here on earth—and why are we in so much trouble? Why are we "in danger every hour?" (1 Cor 15:32). Death is like a giant lion, seeking whom it may devour. I could die at any moment. I live in fear! Pastor Richmann started his theology of the cross with just this situation. He cleverly put it in terms of a strange, unnecessary tradition that began in Medieval times but has been preserved even among the Reformation churches—called Ash Wednesday. The act of meeting at a church on a particular calendar day (yearly, no less) to prepare for Christ's holy suffering and resurrection (which has already happened) is indeed strange. It is also unnecessary for faith. Yet, for all of that, it is a worthwhile exercise to "stretch" faith by having a preacher kill the old sinner and raise the new saint. Paul says this will happen repeatedly: "I die every day!" (1 Cor 15:31).

Paul even says, "But someone will ask, 'How are the dead raised? With what kind of body do they come?" (1 Cor 15:35). Fool! Faith doesn't see yet, in the same way that a farmer doesn't see the corn he planted in the ground. So it is with resurrection; all you see for now is a dead body. You see the casket or the "urn" for those burned to ashes. It is no different from when God first created Adam from the dust of the ground. Do you believe that if we could have seen the red clay-ash of the earth before Adam, we would have said to God, "I see precisely your plan to make a man from this mud"? Get over yourselves, Paul says! Quit thinking with your lying eyes!

Thus, this book begins with the simple religious tradition of placing ashes on someone's forehead. It then opens to the entire theology of the cross that says we are not put on this earth to march toward death (live until you die) but that we die to live! We are not life-to-deathers but death-to-lifers. For this reason, we teach that theology is not just cultivating old traditions but actual, present proclamation. Proclamation accomplishes something that God wants to do, and he wants to do it through his preachers. Paul says, "How will they hear without a preacher?" (Rom 10), and in Isaiah 55, God says, "My word will not return to me empty, but will accomplish what I desire and achieve the purpose for which I sent it."

This book is an excellent example of a purposeful, productive, divine theology that ultimately gives us Christ and him crucified for the forgiveness of our sins. It may seem strange that it begins with Ash Wednesday and his own daughter's questions about placing ashes on the forehead. From this liturgical sign, Pastor Richmann then builds out the entire teaching of creation, sin, the blood of Christ, and our salvation—for where there is forgiveness of sin, there is also life and salvation (*Small Catechism*). He understands that we do not begin, as Christians, with life that moves toward death. We are not in the business of euthanasia: preparing people for making a "good death." We begin with death—ashes—and are made alive: death to life, not life to death. German theologians used to refer to this kind of work as a "*Grundriss*"—an outline or sketch of the entire teaching of the Christian church, from sin and death to resurrection. It is the "meat of the word, not just the milk" (1 Cor 3:2), but it is pounded and tenderized so that it goes down well.

It is like Paul telling his congregation that their bodies are like seeds in the ground. When the shoot comes up, everyone is amazed that out of such dust comes life. All the while, we remember that the very last "sting" of death (Hos 13:14)—the thing that makes us deny death and deny our bodies—is sin: "The sting of death is sin" (1 Cor 15:56a). Sin is the problem it is because of the power of the law: "The power of sin is the law" (1 Cor 15:56b). God gave the law to denounce sin, and in condemning sin, the law's power was to give the death penalty to sin. Sin's "stinger" (as Pastor Richmann says) is death. There is no denying that truth. But do you know what? God gave not only the law but his Son Jesus Christ—and "God gives us the victory [over sin, death, and the devil] through our Lord Jesus

Christ" (1 Cor 15:57). When Christ was raised from the dead, he declared victory over the sin that had stung him on the cross—and over the law that empowered death's sting. Once Christ has conquered, all our troubles come to an end: sin, death, and the law are no more.

Once you know that, you can be "stretched" by God and carry on for now, "steadfast, immovable, always abounding in God's work, understanding that in the Lord, your troubles are not empty" (1 Cor 15:58). Your troubles and stretchings are not self-emptying (kenotic) as Christ's (Phil 2) were, but neither are they useless. They are firming your faith and making you worthy to preach this gospel to another sinner—and it works! You raise the dead just as you have been raised. Enjoy this theological explanation of Ash Wednesday. It is a profound exposition of Paul's 1 Corinthians 15 on death and resurrection, and thus a summary of all theology. A human tradition (ashes) wrapped itself around a living word from Christ, who has already conquered all our enemies. Let this knowledge stretch you from the ashes of Lent to the resurrection of Christ and so of your own body.

—Steven D. Paulson

Senior Scholar-in-Residence, 1517

Introduction

"She was asking me about the ashes," my wife said to me bluntly as we discussed our plans for the next day's Ash Wednesday service. The "she" my wife was referring to was my then four-year-old daughter, whom I had just finished tucking in with our nightly ritual of the Lord's Prayer, reading from Martin Luther's *Small Catechism*, and a few chapters from the crude *Dog Man* comic series—the bedtime combination of faith formation and silliness that all devout Christian parents must learn to make peace with. "And she wants to be the one to put the ashes on you," my wife continued.

I could tell from my wife's tone that she was not just giving me information. She was telling me I had work to do. I needed to find the words to explain to my daughter why every year in late winter people in our church lined up before me to receive ashes smudged on their forehead in the sign of the cross. I also needed to coach her on how to do this: Dip your thumb in the ashes in the bowl, use the ashes to make a cross sign, and say, "Remember you are dust, and to dust you shall return."

We would be observing this holy day as a family of three the same way we had all three years before, and the same way my wife and I had for eight years before our daughter was born. We would be worshiping at the small, rural Lutheran church where I served as pastor.

By this point, my daughter had observed the ritual of the ashes—and received the ashes—a few times that she could remember. She always saw her mom applying the ashes on my forehead after I had done the same for the worshipers who came forward. She was clearly noticing the world around her, seeing that this was an important event, and she wanted to be more involved.

I'll skip over what exactly I said to my daughter the next day to help her understand this ritual and its meaning, since that will be the subject of a later chapter. But suffice it to say that one of the proudest moments of my life as a father was when my daughter, on a dark early March evening in a country Texas church, in front of about twenty fellow believers, with the seriousness of an artist, dipped her thumb in the ashes, marked my forehead with the cross, and reminded me that I would someday die. What was a joy to me in that moment was not that she was dutifully performing the role of pastor's kid, but that she had entered more deeply and more personally into the rich theological tradition that is Lent.

Some Christians can't imagine practicing their faith without Lent, the forty days of somber spirituality that each year precedes Easter. As an annual event lasting several weeks, it is a palpable downbeat in the spiritual rhythms of the year, and it provides much-needed extended religious focus. As an intentionally solemn time leading up to Easter, it makes the celebration of the resurrection that much more joyful. In general, those churches that prize a sense of connection with believers of the past are the ones who observe Lent most "religiously"—although they do not all observe the season the same way. In this group, we would put Catholic, Orthodox (Greek,

Russian, and others), Coptic, Anglican, Episcopal, Lutheran, and some Presbyterians and Methodists.

Other Christians are only vaguely (or not at all) aware of Lent. These are, generally speaking, Christians who take a more suspicious posture toward the past, sensitive to unhealthy and exploitative practices that have harmed believers throughout history. These are typically Baptist, non-denominational, and other evangelical believers. To varying degrees, these Christians have dispensed with traditional practices of the Catholic Church. For them, Lent is in the same category as seeking the intercession of dead saints—a Catholic practice with no biblical support that must be rejected. They are the followers (in spirit if not in fact) of sixteenth-century Swiss reformer Ulrich Zwingli, who famously made his stance against the Catholic Church's Lenten mandates by openly defending those who had eaten sausage during the season when meat was forbidden. Despite this lineage, many evangelicals today are increasingly interested in historic liturgical (that is, scripted worship) practices, including, especially, Lent, perhaps as an antidote to the shallowness and alienation that can come with an overly individualistic spirituality.[1]

Whether you faithfully observe Lent every year or have only recently become curious about it, this book is for you.

---

[1] Chris Gehrz, "When Did Evangelicals Start Observing Lent?," *Anxious Bench* (blog), February 20, 2018, https://www.patheos.com/blogs/anxiousbench/2018/02/evangelicals-lent/; Nicole Alcindor, "Is Lent Becoming More Popular among Evangelicals?," The Christian Post, April 11, 2022, https://www.christianpost.com/news/is-lent-becoming-more-popular-among-evangelicals.html. Accessed November 30, 2023.

Where Did Lent Come From?

Jesus did not observe Lent. And we have no direct evidence of any of Jesus' disciples observing Lent or giving instructions on its observance. In other words, Lent has nothing structurally biblical about it. But to say that Scripture does not precisely spell out a teaching or practice is not to say that it is *unscriptural* or even spiritually unhealthy. Rather, it simply means that we judge its usefulness by scriptural principles. To do this, it helps to know something about the origins of the teaching or practice and the ways it tends to shape and reflect people's ideas about God and the Christian life. What follows is a very brief explanation of the origins of Lent. For history nerds, I've given more details in the Appendix.

Despite the outsized importance of Christmas in American culture today, the day of Jesus' resurrection is more important historically than the day of his birth.[2] As the New Testament tells us, Jesus rose from the dead on a Sunday. Christians almost immediately gravitated to this day of the week as the preferred day for worship, each Sunday being a mini celebration of Christ's resurrection. And early on, the joy of Christ's defeat of death contrasted with more gloomy days of fasting on Wednesdays and Fridays in remembrance of Jesus' betrayal and crucifixion. Because Jesus' resurrection also overlapped with the annual Jewish festival of Passover, it made sense to celebrate Christ's resurrection not only weekly, but also every year around the same time. And again, believers balanced the delight of the resurrection with days of mournful fasting before it—first

[2] Throughout this book, the United States is my primary cultural reference point. I do not intend to exclude or minimize other cultures but to relate the theology of Lent to the culture I know best.

just a few days, then as time went on, a full week of fasting preceded Easter Sunday in some places. Eventually, believer's imaginations were taken with the notion that the pre-Easter fast should last forty days, an echo of Jesus fasting in the wilderness. Because the church regarded Sundays as "feast" days by default, they could not be used in the calculation. Consequently, a forty-day fast leading up to Easter began on Wednesday of the seventh week before Resurrection Sunday.

The theological gravity of Easter (Romans 4:25 says that Christ was "raised for our justification") brought two other practices into its orbit. Before infant baptism became the norm, the church often received converts to Christianity by baptizing them on Easter. They were, in effect, dying and rising with Christ (see Rom 6:4). Over time, the church also gained experience with flagrant sinners or those who renounced the faith wanting to return. The church opted for forgiveness but also required public repentance before receiving them back into the fold in the days just before Easter. Based on biblical examples, this repentance often included putting ashes on one's body or face. Eventually, this practice spread to all Christians in Western Europe, so that Lent began for all with the observance of Ash Wednesday. This tradition of ashes on the Wednesday beginning Lent has continued strong for a thousand years, eventually including me, my wife, and my curious daughter.

Lent: A Collision of Theological Truths

I do not write this book to convince you to observe Lent. Although I think there are good reasons to participate in recurring shared worship practices that have a long pedigree in the church, the real gift of

Lent is that it brings together so many important theological truths. These truths are certainly not the entirety of Christian faith, but they address inescapable realities for those saved by grace through faith.

I'm not trying to have a unique or novel take on Lent; that would probably be at odds with the spirit of Lent, anyway. So, although academic works in history and theology have shaped my ideas (and I'll point to some of these in footnotes), this book is much more the fruit of my pastoral experience. Every year, I return with my congregation to the season of Lent. Coming between the awe of Christmas-Epiphany and the triumph of Easter, this dark season can feel like a long, unnecessary independent clause in the sentence that is the liturgical year. But the longer I serve in public ministry, the more I appreciate that what we confront intentionally and systematically in Lent are the vital arteries of the Christian life in all seasons. Reflecting on one of these themes more than five hundred years ago, Martin Luther insisted that the "entire life of the believer is one of repentance." The same applies to the other Lenten themes I explore in this book: death, denial, temptation, and good works.

By quoting Luther, I show my theological cards. I was baptized and confirmed in Lutheran churches. I am an ordained Lutheran minister. But I was not always a Lutheran. For nearly a decade, coinciding perfectly with my teenage years, I considered myself a Pentecostal or charismatic Christian. And although I circled back to Lutheranism in early adulthood, I will eternally be grateful to God for my years in evangelical and charismatic communities. To be sure, I have left behind many of the beliefs and practices that are common in those communities. But I will forever maintain that it was in a Pentecostal church that the Holy Spirit made the gospel click for me in a way that, for whatever reason, it had not before—that Christ died for *my* sins.

To the extent that any church proclaims such good news, it is because they find it in Scripture. The Bible belongs to all Christians. In what follows, I will often cite Luther or Lutheran documents. But I do this not to be partisan or to try to persuade readers to become Lutheran. Rather, I do this because I believe that the Lutheran movement is, at its best, particularly clear on how we move from reading Scripture to preaching the gospel. As such, thinking "with" Luther and other Lutherans has become my theological habit. But that habit means at the same time always thinking with Scripture, and you'll see this in the chapters that follow.[3]

Although the church never officially worked out its theology of Lent, the themes of this season demonstrate a remarkable coherence. I believe this is because of the church's historic reliance upon Scripture for its language of worship. In other words, God's word is clear that one cannot understand death without understanding self-denial, repentance, temptation, or good works; and this holds true for each theme in relation to all the others. Although it is rarely stated this way, I contend that a common thread in these themes is that in each of these experiences, we are describing ways that God *acts upon us*.

For some, this may seem to turn Lent on its head. With all the talk of repentance, fasting, and good works, one can easily get the impression that of all the seasons of the church year, this one is about

[3] For an accessible primer on the Lutheran approach to Scripture, see Timothy J. Wengert, *Word of Life: Introducing Lutheran Hermeneutics* (Minneapolis: Fortress, 2019).

what *we* do. Even when thinking about temptation, the emphasis seems to be on what we must do to resist, overcome, or avoid it. But when we explore the Scriptures that address these themes and view them in the light of the gospel, we find more going on. In the ways God creates us and continually maintains our lives, we are dependent creatures; this is all the more so when it comes to our redemption. We are clay in the divine potter's hands (Jer 18:1-11; Isa 64:8). As Luther testified, all believers will suffer God's ongoing work, which Luther described graphically as being "stretched out with Christ."[4] The word "stretch" has many shades of meaning. On one hand, we might say we are "stretched too thin" when we have an unhealthy amount of stress in our lives. On the other hand, we might say "that really stretched me" to describe an experience that helped us grow. But what Luther had in mind with this word is profound vulnerability, suffering what is done to us by another, with no defenses—just like Christ on the cross. As a description of the Christian life, "stretched" is a fitting way to approach Lent: the time of year when the days are stretched is an excellent metaphor for the ways God stretches us. To hint at the themes of the following chapters, we confess that it is God who kills and makes alive, imposes fasts, tests faith, gives repentance, and brings forth good deeds out of repentance. When it comes to God's actions upon us, we may often be conscious of this "stretching," and we may even experience it as growth. But that doesn't change the fact

---

[4] Martin Luther, *Luther's Works*, ed. Jaroslav Pelikan and Helmut T. Lehmann (Philadelphia: Fortress; St. Louis: Concordia, 1955), 31:129. Hereafter cited as LW. Cited in Timothy J. Wengert, "'Peace, Peace...Cross, Cross': Reflections on How Martin Luther Relates the Theology of the Cross to Suffering," *Theology Today* 59, no. 2 (July 2002): 195.

that it is suffering in the truest sense, and we are never in control or command of the many ways God reconciles himself to his enemies in Christ's death and resurrection.

How to Read this Book

This book is meant to be interactive. I mean three things by this. First, I invite you to engage actively with the words on the page. As I mentioned above, I will be referring to Scripture a lot. I do this because my own logic is inseparable from the impression that Scripture has made on me. But I also do it because I want to turn readers more deeply into God's word for themselves. You will find that I often refer to scriptural passages; when you see these references in the text, look them up for yourself (for instance, did you look up the Jeremiah or Isaiah passages I just noted above?). Read what comes before and after the passage I quote. Soak yourself in the claims of Scripture. In other places, I ask you to read longer passages and respond to questions, informed by your own experience and your reading of the Scripture. You will profit most from this book if you read it with an open Bible next to you and a notebook to record your responses. I also encourage you, if time permits, to use those places in the chapter with questions as an opportunity to step away from the book, let your mind wander, and ruminate on what you've read thus far. Read this book not like a task to be accomplished but like visits with a friend where you can calmly pick up the conversation right where you left off.

The second way to interact with this book is in the discussion questions at the end of each chapter. Again, you'll get the most out of these questions by recording your responses in a notebook. But these questions are going to be especially useful for stimulating discussion with fellow believers. Although you can certainly get much from this book by reading it on your own, the experience will be richer if you read each chapter and then gather regularly with others—say, in a weekly meeting with a close friend, small group gathering, adult education, or Sunday school—to reflect together. In fact, such discussion in community with other saints may well provide occasions for God to speak his grace to you—an experience that is more likely to occur when the gracious word is audible than when it remains as text on a page (as Paul said, faith comes by hearing, Rom 10:17). The end-of-chapter questions can provide concrete starting points for such discussion, but you can also use the other reflection prompts sprinkled through the chapter and your own reactions to and questions about what you've read.

The final interactive feature of this book appears in the meditations that close each chapter. These concise paragraphs have two purposes. First, they are summaries of the chapter. Coming at the end, they are meant to help you come away with the chapter's main points. Second, they are intended to help you ponder the truths of the chapter in more depth. By reading the concluding meditation slowly many times, over time, writing it out multiple times in your notebook, or even memorizing and reciting it, you will likely come to greater appreciation of that Lenten theme.

My desire is that, by using the astonishing themes of Lent, this book would lead you more deeply into the fundamental truth that God is in control of all things. This truth might look good on paper, but in reality, it can be discomforting and distressing. The fact is, we want to be in control. This is as true in our personal finances as it is in our spiritual journeys. But once we learn the depths of human sin, we begin to see how self-destructive it would be to be in control. When we take up the task of making ourselves something God can love, not only do we delude ourselves that we have this control, but we inevitably wind up creatures destined for wrath. But when God works upon us through the gospel of Jesus Christ, he forms beings bound for life and salvation.

Get ready now to learn how God stretches you.

• CHAPTER ONE •

DUST

The season of Lent begins with death. The day that starts it all, Ash Wednesday, is as dark and somber as its name implies. Christian worshipers across the globe begin their Lent, the great on-ramp to the celebration of life at Easter, with a morbid reminder of death. The climax of the worship service involves the congregants approaching the pastor (or the pastor's assistant) to have ashes smeared on their foreheads in the shape of a cross while hearing the words "Remember you are dust, and to dust you shall return." For those who attend an early morning service, the smudgy cross symbol wears throughout the day, itself gradually dying as wind, sweat, and unconscious touching fade the mark.

It is counterintuitive, of course, that anything could *begin* with death. Apart from God's word, human wisdom can only see death as an end, not a beginning—why else would we resist death and all the signs of aging that remind us of it? But this is one reason Lent is so helpful. For in our state of sin, death must come before life. Put another way, it's not just Lent but the Christian life itself that begins with death.

To dust you shall return—the words speak for themselves. A few eccentric thinkers may have high hopes for "transhumanism," the view that we can eventually overcome our limitations by merging with technology. But such dreams only seem to point to our collective anxieties about death. We know what our destiny is. Do we really need the reminder that we will return to dust? Those who don't observe Lent still often hear the same words at funerals, where, staring at the casket, no one can escape at least a passing thought of his own mortality. But the words are not just an eloquent way to remind us of "the way of all flesh," nor are they some liturgical version of the misguided mantra, "eat, drink, and be merry, for tomorrow we die." They are God's own words, spoken to humans at some distance from the moment of their creation. This should clue us into the fact that something unnatural is happening here. To understand it, however, we need to start with the scene of creation. This will help us see more clearly God's original intent and where things went wrong.

Dirt and Wind

Genesis 1 gives the wide-angle view of creation. Day follows day as God shapes and fills the heavens and the earth. What was once formless now has distinctions—waters above and waters below, sea and dry land. What was empty now hosts birds in the air, fish in the sea, creatures on the land. God accomplishes all by his word, "Let there be…" This is as if to say that in this thirty-thousand-foot view, the method of God's creating is less important than the truth that creation comes into existence as the simple result of God's will.

In Genesis 2, however, we get a telescoped perspective on the story of creation. And the lens is focused on humans. Here we have a ground-level vantage point, and the subject filling the shot is humanity. It is as though the Holy Spirit wanted to make the details of our creation absolutely clear so that we wouldn't get any silly ideas. This story tells us precisely how humans were fashioned, brought to life, and related to the rest of creation and God himself.

Read Genesis 2:4-9 and write your responses to these questions:

1. How does God make man?
2. How does man become alive?
3. What does this story suggest about humanity's relationship to the rest of creation? What does it suggest about humanity's relationship to God?

"The LORD God formed man from the dust of the ground" (v7). God did not make humans from anything special. Neither are they made from something deplorable, like the carcass of a defeated deity (as in ancient Babylonian myths) or the invention of demonic forces (as in early Christianity's rivals, Gnosticism and Manichaeism). They are made of dirt—plain, unassuming, real, and "good" (as all else that God created was *good*). On one hand, it might not seem fitting for humans, the crown of God's creation, to be composed of what we wipe off our feet before entering a house. On the other hand, we demonstrate our acceptance of this truth when we applaud the virtue of *humility* (not coincidentally, often at funerals); for humility is literally being connected to the ground. As we might say of a humble person, "she was really *grounded*." We mean it as a complement when we describe someone as "down to earth." In fact, the word *human* is directly related to *humility* and shows the same wordplay as the word "Adam" coming from the Hebrew word for "dust" or "earth."

"[God] breathed into his nostrils the breath of life; and the man became a living being" (v7). The man does not have life "by right" or by definition. Life comes from outside, and the human receives it as a gift. The human—such as he is before the breath of God entered his nostrils—waits passively to be enlivened by God's wind. He is totally dependent. To be sure, there is something special in this arrangement. The breath is divine. Imagine God crouching over the man-shaped dirt pile, giving him mouth-to-mouth suscitation.

Read carefully, this story challenges our assumptions about human nature. We generally imagine that humans are composed of at least two "parts" or "aspects." More specifically, we take for granted that humans have a self-aware immortal part (a "soul" or perhaps a "spirit"), in contrast to the mortal part, the body. But this is foreign not only to the Genesis story but to the Old Testament picture of humanity. Scripture tells us that the "spirit" in humans is not properly *their* spirit but *God's Spirit*. This is the life force of humanity, and it is not a part of human nature. Rather, it is on loan from God. As Ecclesiastes 12:7 says, "the spirit returns to God who gave it." Job's otherwise dense friend Elihu had this much right:

If [God] should take back his spirit to himself,
    and gather to himself his breath,
all flesh would perish together,
    and all mortals return to dust. (Job 34:14-15)

And he echoes the psalmist:

when you take away their breath, they die
    and return to their dust.
When you send forth your spirit, they are created;
    and you renew the face of the ground. (Ps 104:29-30)

Our misconceptions about how humans were created for this life ties directly to our misconceptions about the afterlife. Many Christians believe that eternal life is our disembodied soul enjoying direct spiritual communion with God. This theology is reflected in such beloved hymns as "I'll Fly Away." In fact, when I ask my undergraduate students (who have all taken a semester-long course on Christian Scriptures) how the Bible characterizes the afterlife, about a third agree with the statement, "After the body dies, a disembodied soul lives forever with God." But Scripture—both Old and New Testaments—speaks of a re-formed and resuscitated body—in other words, the creation 2.0. This was the orthodox Christian teaching for several centuries after Christ: Humans always live—whether in this life or the next—as bodies enlivened by God's breath.[1] To be sure, the second body of believers is of a different "glory" than the first, as Paul says in 1 Corinthians 15. This new body is

[1] Nancey Murphy, "Immortality versus Resurrection in the Christian Tradition," *Annals of the New York Academy of Sciences* 1234 (October 2011): 76–82, https://doi.org/10.1111/j.1749-6632.2011.06132.x.

imperishable—but it is imperishable not because it is innately immortal but because it is eternally born from "a life-giving spirit," that is, Christ. These are the dry bones Ezekiel was commanded to prophesy, "I will cause breath to enter you, and you will live" (Ezek 37:5). This body is immortal because in the resurrection it "puts on" immortality.

Words, Worship, and Trees

But to speak of resurrection is to get ahead of ourselves. First, we must know why humanity needs *re*suscitating in the first place. And that brings us to the words God spoke to Adam (and Adam passed on to Eve) to shape the human life of ceaseless worship. In this way, God established the church itself, even before family or government.

> Read Genesis 2:15-17 and write your responses to these questions:
>
> 1. What does God give man?
> 2. What does God forbid man?
> 3. What is the consequence of doing what is forbidden?

The two divine words came in the form of a gift and a prohibition, both of which God placed into a tree. The gift was not stingy; it was free range of the entire garden: "You may freely eat of every tree of the garden" (v16). This lavish gift included the tree of life. Adam and Eve worshiped God by partaking of his free gift, by receiving God where he bid them to receive him. Such worship was life. The fruit of this tree preserved Adam and Eve in perfect health and vitality. The tree of life was the real fountain of youth.

But another word-and-tree combination existed alongside the gift: "of the tree of the knowledge of good and evil you shall not eat" (v17). The humans were to worship God not only by tearing into the fruit he had given but also by refraining from devouring what God had not given. True worship entailed Adam and Eve standing at the foot of this tree, respecting and revering God precisely by not eating from it. To be sure, all that God created—including the tree of the knowledge of good and evil—was good. This tree was not some kind of natural poison any more than the tree of life was a natural elixir of vitality. Both trees became to Adam what they were because of God's word attached to them, much like Moses' bronze serpent in the wilderness restored the Israelites (Num 21:9). Historically, Christians have used the word "sacrament" to describe this intimate association of God's word with a physical thing. We could say that the trees in the Garden were sacramental, and we see that Adam's experience was not that far removed from our own, although the shape of the sacrament and its immediate effects are different for us. The humans were forbidden from seeking divinity in anything but the grace of God.

The prohibition came with a warning. We could call it a threat of punishment, but it is deeper than that and not so transactional as the word *punishment* implies. We hear it in the words, "in the day that you eat of [the tree of the knowledge of good and evil] you shall die" (v17). But a closer translation would render God's words as "in the day of your eating of it, *dying you shall die.*" This is not just a matter of emphasis (make no mistake, you *will* die!), although that is part of it. But the doubled verb (*dying...die*) reveals that death is what happens not simply as a result of eating the forbidden fruit but *in the act* of eating the fruit.

Read Genesis 3 and write your responses to these questions:

1. What knowledge do the man and woman gain after eating the forbidden fruit?
2. What are the curses God pronounces?
3. Why does God drive the man and woman out of the Garden?

You likely know how the story goes. In later chapters, we will explore what was "wrong" with the humans' actions. For now, we simply need to rehearse the events. Eve listens to the serpent, eats the forbidden fruit, and offers it to Adam, who also partakes. When Adam comes clean to God about their rebellion, God pronounces a series of curses disturbing the fundamental vocations of human life. God pronounces pain and disorder in childbearing (3:16). This is broader, of course, than the physical pain of giving birth. In our modern world, we might think we have outsmarted this curse with the use of an epidural. But this curse is also about child*rearing,* and we have invented no epidural for that pain, encompassing everything from postpartum depression to the hurtful things children say to their parents to the late nights spent worrying when children are out with friends. And God's curse also extends to work (3:17-18). Work was originally pure joy, but now, work is toil and frustration. The farmer knows lean harvests despite backbreaking labor; the white-collar worker knows the demoralizing effects of toxic office politics, with self-important coworkers sabotaging meetings and bosses playing favorites. In short, these curses bring suffering into the picture of what God calls humans to do. The peace and harmony of the Garden are lost.

As undeniable as these curses are, since they so accurately describe human life now under the dominion of sin, they are not directly related to the original warning. So, then comes the whopper curse: "you are dust, and to dust you shall return" (3:19). This was the first Ash Wednesday. Here God instituted a liturgy that continues to this day. The story of Adam's and Eve's rebellion is not just an origin story. It is the story of original sin, the story of originating sin, the story of all sin, including yours. As many—including twentieth-century theologian Reinhold Niebuhr—have said, "The doctrine of original sin is the only empirically verifiable doctrine of the Christian faith."[2] Take a moment to reflect on the world around you as well as your own thoughts, words, and deeds. Greed extends from Wall Street to adult children bickering over inheritance. Unfaithfulness stretches from crooked politicians to millions of broken marriages. The evidence of humanity's rebellion against God is overwhelming.

We always seem to be trying to wriggle out of the clear meaning of this text, importing ideas about human immortality, temptation, and free will. But Scripture gives us several important commentaries, including 1 Corinthians 15 and Romans 5, that unflinchingly lay the

[2] Andrew S. Finstuen, *Original Sin and Everyday Protestants: The Theology of Reinhold Niebuhr, Billy Graham, and Paul Tillich in an Age of Anxiety* (Chapel Hill: University of North Carolina Press, 2009), 69.

meaning of Adam's and Eve's sin upon us. In the Old Testament, the central rumination on Genesis 3 is Psalm 90. Here the psalmist reminds us of the Ash Wednesday curse, "You turn us back to dust" (v3). Psalm 90 is really the entry point into all the books of Moses (Genesis-Deuteronomy) and is truly a "prayer of Moses" as the traditional title indicates.

> Read Psalm 90 and write your responses to these questions:
>
> 1. What echoes do you hear of Genesis 3?
> 2. What about this Psalm makes it especially appropriate to be associated with Moses?
> 3. What does this Psalm suggest about what humans can expect in life?

Wrath and Death

As any fan of Charlton Heston in *The Ten Commandments* knows, Moses is not just the "man of God" but preeminently the man of the *law*. And to know God's law is to know its effects, especially God's wrath. When we have Moses teaching that "we are consumed by your anger; by your wrath we are overwhelmed" (v7) this is, as Martin Luther memorably put it, "Moses at his most Mosaic."[3] Of course, no one today talks about God's wrath, at least not in polite company. Nothing could be less fashionable than suggesting that God burns with white hot anger against any human he created. It seems the only

[3] LW 13:77.

people willing to speak of God's wrath are unhinged televangelists pontificating, for instance, why earthquakes or floods hit certain parts of the globe.

Our allergy to the notion of God's wrath is an inheritance of liberal theology, a development in elite European nineteenth-century Christianity that was certain that God's definitive attribute is love and God reveals his love and providence through the steady progress of human cultural development and achievements. In the shadow of liberal theology, many Christians were left with what H. Richard Niebuhr (Reinhold's brother) famously summarized: "A God without wrath brought men without sin into a kingdom without judgment through the ministrations of a Christ without a cross."[4]

Niebuhr aptly criticized the pitfalls of liberal theology, particularly its handling of God's wrath. It was only by surgically removing any lingering commitment to Scripture that such a wrathless theology could flourish. Regardless of where you start reading, you will not get far in Scripture without encountering stories of God's wrath. After the sin of Adam and Eve, God's wrath is directed toward all creation in the Flood, to the specific populations of Sodom and Gomorrah, to the Egyptian enslavers of God's chosen Israel, and to Israel itself both during their wilderness travels and while inhabiting the Promised Land.

Although many of these stories are familiar and create the popular image of the "God of the Old Testament" as the angry version of God in the Bible, the writers of the New Testament quite self-consciously carry forward the message of God's wrath. One of the best

---

[4] H. Richard Niebuhr, *The Kingdom of God in America* (New York: Harper, 1959), 193.

preachers of God's wrath is John the Baptist. For him, God's wrath is first and foremost an impending phenomenon that you can only hope to escape through repentance and faith in God's coming one, Jesus Christ. In both Matthew and Luke, John the Baptist castigates his Jordan River audience as a "brood of vipers," and he charges them, "who warned you to flee the wrath to come?" (Matt 3:7; Luke 3:7). In John 3, just a few verses after Jesus' famous claim of God's love for the world, the Baptizer makes it clear that "Whoever believes in the Son has eternal life; whoever disobeys the Son will not see life, but must endure God's wrath" (v36).

Other New Testament voices make clear that God's wrath is more than a looming event. For the apostle Paul, God's wrath is an inescapable reality of human life. Paul tells the believers in Ephesus that "All of us once...were by nature children of wrath, like everyone else" (Eph 2:3). For this reason, writes Paul in Romans, "the wrath of God is revealed from heaven against all ungodliness and wickedness of those who by their wickedness suppress the truth" (1:18). We can make the New Testament case for God's wrath even without Jesus' own words regarding "weeping and gnashing of teeth" of the wicked and the carnage of the book of Revelation.

But trying to prove God's wrath by scriptural proof-texting is surely to miss the point. The truth is, people everywhere, every day, feel God's wrath—and not as merely an afterlife threat but as a present reality. The problem is they either don't have the name for it, or they are committed to denying that it is what it is. Psalm 90 calls a thing what it is. God's wrath is felt in our daily toil: "all our days pass away under your wrath" (v9). If we have ears to hear, the dangers and pains of life are trying to tell us something—we are sinful, and God is angry. When suffering friends or family members confess to us a fear that God is angry with them (often expressed in the psalmist's lament sensing God's *absence*, "Why do you hide your face from me?"),[5] we too often swoop in with unbiblical platitudes to excuse God of wrath, like "God doesn't give you more than you can handle," or "What doesn't kill you makes you stronger." But even before God pronounced official curses, Adam and Eve experienced the sad results of their sin—they feared the sound of God's footsteps (Gen 3:8-9). Once sin enters the picture, God's law is no longer simply a directive for proper worship but becomes an agent of terror that causes fright at the sound of rustling leaves. Our minds run wild, imagining the vicious animal or thug causing the noise. But beneath that fear lies the deeper sense of God's wrath.

Occasionally, a sinner will confess this very thing. Recently, I was counseling a parishioner who wanted to have his two children baptized. He had not had his girls baptized as infants (which we often do as Lutherans), so I asked him why he was considering this now. He proceeded to tell me that a series of deaths in his family had made him feel like he had a target on his back. Several near-misses with falling ceiling fans convinced him that some dangerous force was out to get him. Getting his girls baptized was the beginning of an attempt to address the fear. Within the jumble of emotions this man experienced, he clearly felt God's wrath. As unpleasant as it is, he is not wrong. In fact, no one who senses God's wrath is ever wrong, as such; although believing that this is God's *ultimate* attitude toward you leads to despair and hell. As I tell my congregation frequently, to determine if some experience is God's wrath, we start with the "duck test." If it walks

[5] See, for example, Psalms 13, 44, and 88.

like a duck, looks like a duck, and quacks like a duck, it is probably a duck. Things go bump in the night. We lose sleep over the stock market. People die around us left and right. We end up gaslighting all of humanity by trying to tell people they are not experiencing God's wrath when they know in their bones—if not their brains—that they are. Yet, in the end, the pastoral question is not whether some experience is evidence of God's wrath but what can be done in the face of God's wrath. Thankfully, in Christ, something *is* done, which does not merely avoid or deny God's wrath but ends it forever. But before we get to that, we must explore further the consequences of human sin.

Death and Nature

God's curse on Adam and Eve clearly places humans under God's wrath as they live their lives in this valley of sorrow. But the curse is also, crucially, a matter of death. In his wrath, God *consumes* and *overwhelms* us (Ps 90:7). As humans in the mold of the rebellious first couple, we return to dust. All of humanity is powerless in the face of God's death sentence.

In teaching death, I ask folks first to answer the question, "Is death a natural aspect of human existence?" The initial consensus is always that, yes, death is natural. I'm not surprised by this response, since it is common to see death as a natural part of life. The ex-Beatle George Harrison famously sang "All things must pass away," and "all things" certainly includes human life. It is an ancient perspective, with roots in the so-called wisdom traditions of both the East and the West. And if you consider your own experience, you don't have any evidence to refute it. Not only does every day turn to nightfall and every summer give way to autumn, but every human eventually turns to dust. It doesn't matter how much you love them, whether they are young or old, or how much good they do in the world. The death of each person we know seems to reinforce the message that the experience of death is universal. And it seems that the best way to make sense of it is to label it "natural."

But this view of death-as-natural deserves closer scrutiny. In our day, it is mostly the medical community (including psychology) that feeds us this line.[6] Despite its scientific trappings, the view that death is natural is actually a belief that can't be proven by science or reason. In that sense, it is a *myth*.[7] But I have encountered this philosophy nearly everywhere people discuss death, including from presenters in pastoral training events. The motivation for this teaching can be noble; for instance, helping families of a fatally ill loved one allow the last moments to be moments of peace and reconciliation rather than fighting against the inevitable with multiplying medications, therapies, and hail-Mary procedures.

In my pastoral work, I have sat with many families in the hospital or home gathered around a dying loved one. They are often either weighing, or justifying after the fact, a decision to forego some treatment that had a chance of prolonging their loved one's life. In convincing themselves of the logic that would willingly let their beloved die, they often reach for the thought that death is natural. In cases where the loved one experienced significant pain, they may even welcome death as a relief. The rot under the surface of such sentiments is that they attempt

[6] Particularly influential is Sherwin B. Nuland, *How We Die: Reflections on Life's Final Chapter* (New York: Vintage, 1993), chaps. 3, 4, 12, Epilogue.

[7] Neil Gillman, *The Death of Death: Resurrection and Immortality in Jewish Thought* (Woodstock, VT: Jewish Lights, 1997), 35.

to defang death; "natural" is another way of saying that death has no moral implication, that it has nothing to say about us as humans. Death is certainly unpleasant but ultimately the way things are, by design.

Humans have always nurtured such methods for trying to neutralize death. Without even appealing to God's promises, people will assert that the dearly departed has "gone to a better place," assuming that death is by nature a refuge of some kind. Often, people who say such things are trying to dull the blunt edge of sorrow. Death, of course, is scary, and it is no wonder that we try to put a positive spin on it. Stop and consider what you have said and heard at funerals. What were the motivations behind these words? What is the attitude toward death revealed in these words? In a very different context, soldiers and those who lead them work hard to convince themselves that death is glorious when it is for the right cause—perhaps the "fatherland," or more abstractly "freedom" and "democracy." In a different bid to deny the reality of death, the beloved poem "Immortality" asserts that humans live on in nature:

> Do not stand
> By my grave, and weep.
> I am not there,
> I do not sleep—
> I am the thousand winds that blow
> I am the diamond glints in snow[8]

Ditties like this show clearly how desperate humans are to deny death, inventing baseless assertions to pull the wool over our own eyes as we face mortality.

---

[8] Clare Harner, "Immortality," *The Gypsy*, December 1934; repr., *AllPoetry*, accessed June 16, 2025, https://allpoetry.com/poem/8498493-Immortality-by-Clare-Harner.

While some try to neutralize death by befriending or belittling it, others try to deny that death holds overwhelming power over humans. We see this often in popular fiction, TV, and film. Whether the hoped-for source of perpetual life is some secret feature of nature (*Tuck Everlasting* [2002], *The Fountain* [2006]) or futuristic technology that can retain or transfer consciousness when a body expires (*Self/less* [2015], *Altered Carbon* [2018-2020], *Upload* [2020-]), our entertainment commonly features the notion that humans can somehow crack the code of death. Hollywood's habits aside, the quest for immortality is as old as humanity itself. Lodged in the earliest literature is the search for some secret knowledge or power to overcome death. Famously, in the Babylonian *Epic of Gilgamesh*, (written at least two thousand years before Christ) the hero-king, driven doubly by his sorrow for his friend's death and the existential crisis that this death thrusts him into, literally travels to the end of the world in a futile attempt to secure eternal life. Returning in his disappointment, Gilgamesh discovers that there is another way to claim immortality: The legacy he left in the building of the city walls would keep "Gilgamesh" alive for generations.

Gilgamesh was displaying what cultural anthropologist Ernest Becker masterfully explored in his Pulitzer Prize-winning *The Denial of Death*.[9] Feeling our own impending deaths, we attach ourselves to symbols of immortality—heroes, causes, and projects that feel *lasting*, even eternal. We may even appeal to our personal contributions to the collective progress of humanity. As expressed in the lyrics of a song by heavy metal band Alter Bridge, "Someday, we'll fade to nothing/...

[9] Ernest Becker, *The Denial of Death* (New York: Simon and Schuster, 1973).

We'll be okay as long as there is something/We can leave behind."[10] Linking to such symbols, we aspire to exist in some way beyond the boundaries of our bodies and limits of our lifespans.

This impulse to live on in what we "leave behind" appears most conspicuously in the human penchant for putting one's name on things. Fathers imprint their names on their firstborn sons. People of wealth inscribe their names on buildings, parks, and awards. Less obviously, we hope to live on in creating things that outlast us. Dedicated professionals commit their final working years to establishing a project, procedure, or platform that will be their "legacy." People strive for awards because others will see their names on plaques and in pamphlets long after they are gone. (One way to think of writing a book is as a hope that the author can keep speaking after he dies.) But none of it is an actual escape from death, as Psalm 49 astutely observes:

> When we look at the wise, they die;
> fool and dolt perish together
> and leave their wealth to others.
> Their graves are their homes for ever,
> their dwelling-places to all generations,
> though they named lands their own. (Ps 49:10-11)

At the heart of this Psalm is the teacher's appraisal of wealth. The verdict is that no amount of wealth, no "ransom," can ensure that "one should live on forever" (v9). As one commentator notes, the writer of this Psalm has "perceived the profound truth that behind the human

---

[10] Alter Bridge, "Season of Promise," track 8 on *Pawns and Kings*, Napalm Records, 2022.

fascination of wealth is a denial of death."[11] It may seem like such *denials* of death are opposite the *acceptance* of death expressed in the sentiment that death is "natural." But both approaches refuse to reckon with the full meaning of death (and I hasten to remind you that at this point we are considering death apart from the hope of Christ, which we'll get to soon). First, in death we are actually done for. A rich tradition of reflection on the finality and hopelessness of *sheol* (the "grave") in the Old Testament drives this point home (for example, Ps 30:9-10, Isa 38:18-19). Second, we die because of God's wrath over our rebellion. Whether we are trying to deny death's power or embrace it as a friend, these are all wicked inventions attempting in vain to escape God's wrath. We are all, collectively, whistling past the graveyard. Knowing precisely what happened in the Garden, Moses makes us face the fact that our death is the result of God's wrath.

Grammatically speaking, this is a simple statement: We die because of God's wrath. But it is not an easy truth to contemplate. It means nothing other than "that God hates us on account of sin," which is surely "an intolerable burden," as Luther noted.[12] Those who are already in the throes of despair or grief should not spend too much time on this without hearing the gospel (see chapter 4, "Turn"). As Luther confessed, he often had to set this Psalm aside when meditating on it in the monastery.[13]

Is all death, then, unnatural? No. As humans are a special and royal creature among all God's creation, so their death is a special

---

[11] James Luther Mays, *Psalms*, Interpretation, a Bible Commentary for Teaching and Preaching (Louisville, KY: John Knox, 1994), 192.

[12] LW 13:106.

[13] LW 13:86.

case. The death of animals may resemble that of humans—similar diseases, decay, and disasters leading to the cessation of heartbeat and breath. But beneath the surface, something very different is happening. Animals die due to the laws of nature. The squirrels in my backyard, my beloved pet cat (shout out to Sonny!), butterflies fluttering in a field—the deaths of all these are natural. Their deaths are part of God's design. Humans, however, were not designed to die, since they were created for eternity. Again, this is not "immortality" in the sense of some quality inherent in humanity's soul or some other divine aspect.[14] God's intent for humanity—for Adam and Eve and their offspring—was to endlessly worship God by reverently abstaining from the tree of the knowledge of good and evil and partaking of the tree of life. They would live eternally as they ate the meal of this tree and by doing so worshiped God as he as desired. But they rebelled, preferring God apart from his gift. God no longer wanted them eating from the tree of life, because in that case, they would "live forever" (v22). Apart from the tree, they die, fulfilling the original threat. So God executed Adam and Eve by banishing them from the Garden.

---

[14] A strident biblical case for the "naturalness" of death is found in James Barr, *The Garden of Eden and the Hope of Immortality* (Minneapolis: Fortress, 1993). Barr goes astray, however, in assuming that immortality as an inherent quality of the human is the only possible form of original human divinely ordained eternal life. Since Genesis does not teach that humans were created with such "immortality," Barr reasons, human death must be natural—that is, intended by God from the beginning. But in fact, Genesis teaches that humans were to live forever by eating from the tree of life. This is precisely the reason Luther preferred to say that humans were created for *eternity*, rather than for *immortality*, although his students seem not to have appreciated this distinction. See LW 13:124, n78.

Destroying Death

Thus far, we have explored death with the texts that the first Christians would have had at hand, that is, the Old Testament. But the first Christians had more than this; they also had God's revelation in Jesus Christ. And with their written witness to that revelation (aka, the New Testament), we can summarize Scripture's teaching, come to a proper regard of death, and point clearly to its solution.

First, we can say clearly what death is. For centuries, theology, taking its cue from Greek philosophy, has described death as the separation of the immortal soul from the mortal body. But as Jewish scholar Neil Gilman says, "the notion of immortality [of the soul] tends to deny the reality of death, of God's power to take my life and to restore it."[15] If, however, death is the process of creating life *in reverse*, from a biblical perspective, death occurs when God's breath (or spirit) departs from the body. Death is the undoing of life that occurs when God breathes his spirit in us, a reversal of creation itself. When God takes stock of human wickedness before the Flood, he says, "My spirit shall not abide in mortals forever" and establishes 120 years as the upper limit of human lifespan (Gen 6:3). We know, for instance, that Jesus' death was a real death because the Gospel writers tell us that he "gave up the spirit" (Matt 27:50; Mark 15:37; Luke 23:46).[16] As God's Spirit withdraws, the body dies and begins its return to dust.

---

[15] Gillman, *The Death of Death*, 238.

[16] This is my literal translation. Most modern translations obscure the mechanics of death by referring to "his" (Jesus') spirit or saying that he "died" or "breathed his last." For my money, you can't improve on the King James Version: "gave up the ghost," but no one uses the word "ghost" anymore to refer to the divine life force within humans.

Second, we must unwaveringly identify the cause of death. We say people die of pneumonia, cancer, and car crashes. Although less common now, we used to read in obituaries that so-and-so died of "natural causes." Scripture shows this to be a lie. After encountering the information in this chapter, congregants who had unanimously agreed that death is a natural aspect of human existence unfailingly reverse their answers when I poll them a second time. Human death may be inevitable, but that is not the same thing as saying it is natural. There is nothing natural in the death of any human; sicknesses and accidents only identify the instrument of a person's death, not its cause. All people die because of God's wrath, and God's wrath is God's response to sin. Whether the death certificate says suicide, blunt trauma, cancer, or pneumonia, the cause is always the same: sin.

This is not to say that we can point to a particular sin causing a particular death. Rather, we confess that we are all born into a world where sin is inescapable, and sin brings death along with it. As Paul says, "the stinger of death is sin" (1 Cor 15:56, translation altered). Sin is the instrument by which death is inflicted on human bodies; sin is the deadly venom of a snake. Or, put another way, "The wages of sin is death" (Rom 6:23). Here, Paul means to tell us that in our rebellion, humans—starting with Adam and Eve—traded a *gift* economy for a *wage* economy (more on this in chapter 5, "Piety"). And in this wage economy, the only thing humans can earn is death, since before God the only thing we have to offer is sin: "all our righteous deeds are like a filthy cloth" (Isa 64:6). Even the best of what we produce is unclean.

Third, we must have the proper attitude toward death. This is where hope comes into this otherwise admittedly grim story. I have not yet explicitly stated what this attitude is, but it follows from the right understanding of death laid out above. Yet it seems that only in the light of Christ's resurrection—that is, his *defeat* of death—can we confess this attitude toward death.[17] For apart from Christ's resurrection, we cannot summon the audacity to defy death, and we are tempted always to domesticate it or make peace with it instead, as we've seen. At this point, Lent bleeds into Easter. Or, better stated, the power of Christ's resurrection is such that Easter cannot be contained to any single day or season of the church calendar.

> Read 1 Corinthians 15:20-57 and write your responses to these questions:
>
> 1. What does Adam's sin condition do to us?
> 2. How should we regard death?
> 3. How does God's law relate to death?
> 4. How does understanding death as God's wrath affect your view of mortality?

In 1 Corinthians 15, Paul explains that death came through a human being, that is, Adam. Just so, the resurrection of the dead comes also through a human being—this time, Jesus Christ. Jesus' resurrection was not a personal victory for his own honor or vindication, it was the "first fruits" of the resurrection of those who belong to Christ. This suggests two things. First, our resurrection is certain, because Christ has been raised. Second, we wait for our resurrection, like a farmer waiting for the fulness of his crop to come

[17] Neil Gillman, a Jewish philosopher, comes very close by referring to death as "incoherent." Gillman, *The Death of Death*, 148–49.

in. We wait not just in this life but also in our death. In that certain waiting experience—both living through the deaths of those around us and living in dread of our own deaths—we come to regard death properly, as the *enemy*. "The last enemy to be destroyed is death," Paul tells us (1 Cor 15:26). This is precisely the passage that I recite every time I officiate at a burial service. In that moment, staring at the dust, the undeniable power of death, we rightly name death as the enemy while also confessing that death does not win. Death is not what God originally wanted for humans, and death will be conquered. At Christ's coming, the perishable will put on imperishability. As Isaiah promised, "death has been swallowed up in victory" (1 Cor 15:54, see Isa 25:8).

At this point, we can say that Christ's resurrection is the "solution" to the problem of human death. That is to speak abstractly, in the realm of ideas. As true as it is, it is of little value. It's like telling someone to be glad that the national economy is strong when that person has been laid off from work and can't pay rent. In the same way, Christ's resurrection doesn't matter unless it also means resurrection for this or that *particular* person. We are understandably concerned about our own fate; this is the unavoidable existential dimension of salvation. And we are also concerned about the fate of others, especially those we know and love; this is what we might call the evangelistic dimension. Based on where our study has carried us thus far, we can put the crucial question like this: If God promises resurrection to an imperishable life for those who belong to Christ, how does one come to belong to Christ?

At the beginning of this chapter, I said that the Christian life begins with death. This is not a slick paradoxical slogan or a kind of Christian koan; it is the central truth of salvation. Scripture spells this out most directly in Romans 6. Here, Paul tells us that "those who have been baptized into Christ Jesus were baptized into his death" (v3). The end of all of this is, of course, eternal life; but first, baptism unites us with Christ's death and means that "our old self was crucified" (v6). Christians, therefore, speak of experiencing not one death but two. You die in baptism, and you die when God's Spirit departs. But the two deaths are not equal. Baptism delivers the liberating, unconditional forgiveness of sins that guarantees our eternal life in righteousness, but just so it is an agonizing death of self that we bitterly resist our whole lives long. Both by comparison and consequence, this makes the physical death when you stop breathing merely a "little" and "gentle" death.[18] This is how Jesus can, in the same breath, tell the grieving sister of Lazarus both that "those who believe in me, even though they die, will live," and that "everyone who lives and believes in me will never die" (John 11:25, 26). Physical death is *undeathed*, stripped of its power and terror because it no longer means that wrath is God's ultimate and lasting attitude toward you.

I suspect this is so little understood because rarely is the biblical logic laid out for us. So let me give it a try.

- By virtue of his resurrection, Christ has the power to unite believers to his death and resurrection in baptism (i.e., your baptism is a real death).

---

[18] Martin Luther, *The Precious and Sacred Writings of Martin Luther: Martin Luther's Epistle Sermons, Trinity Sunday to Advent,* trans. John Nicholas Lenker (Minneapolis: Lutherans in All Lands, 1909), 149, 150, 154.

- God's law has no claim over, and cannot accuse of sin, those who have died (Rom 4:15; 7:4).
- Therefore, you are no longer a sinner.
- God's wrath is aimed only at sinners.
- Since you are not a sinner, God's wrath is no longer aimed at you.
- Therefore, you are freed from death, the preeminent effect of God's wrath.

In short, death is the crucial weapon against death. And it is in that death that new life begins, for baptism unites us not only to Christ's death but also his resurrection.

Concluding Meditation

On Ash Wednesday many Christians mark their foreheads with ashes in the shape of the cross and hear the words, "remember that you are dust and to dust you shall return." This sign has two parts: the ashes and the cross. The ashes are a reminder that humans die because of God's anger at our sin. Our bodies return to ash and dust, and there is nothing we can do about that. But the sign of the cross is a reminder that God has done something about it. God sent his Son Jesus to die on the cross, and his death did not last forever. He rose from the dead. So also it will be for us who belong to Jesus: though we die we will live again with God forever.

QUESTIONS FOR DISCUSSION:

1. How do you react to the suggestion that humans don't necessarily have an immortal soul? Does this make any difference for how you think about human bodies?

2. Knowing that death is not "natural" for humans, how might this change how you think or act when you are dealing with the death of a loved one?

3. In what moments in your life have you sensed God's wrath or God's absence?

4. In what ways do you sense yourself avoiding the meaning of death? Do you try to make death seem less scary? Do you try to outsmart death by focusing on how you will be remembered?

5. Based on your reading of Romans 6, how should you respond when you feel the presence of sin in your life?

6. If you have attended Ash Wednesday services, how has this ritual affected the way you think about death and resurrection?

• CHAPTER TWO •

DENIAL

My first job—if you don't count paper routes and a few weeks in the summer detasseling corn—was at a fast-food restaurant. It was behind the fryer at this burger joint that I first learned about the importance of fish during Lent. As a Midwesterner surrounded by plenty of Catholics, I should have become conscious of this before I was sixteen, but young people have a way of only paying attention to what directly impacts them. Nearly ninety percent of the year, we did not serve fish. But then, suddenly, in late winter, not only would fish appear on the menu, but we were guaranteed to nearly sell out every few days. And then, as quickly as it appeared, the fish disappeared from the menu, and we returned to our regular routine of flipping burgers.

I grew up in Lutheran churches that observed Lent; we sang all the minor key songs, changed the colors in the sanctuary to purple, and gathered for soup suppers on Wednesday evenings. But I never belonged to a congregation that was particularly adamant about fasting during the season. Still, I got a rudimentary education in the Lenten fast when I had to learn how to fry a fish patty.

My experience at the fast-food restaurant helps explain why it is that if there's one thing most people seem to know about Lent, it is that it is a season of fasting. As we saw in the introduction, fasting was the defining practice of pre-Easter observance, even before it developed into the forty days of Lent we know today. The precise details of the fast have always varied among Christians, depending on region and tradition. For some groups, fasting meant eating nothing until sundown; for others it meant abstaining from certain foods only. Over time, these practices solidified into "rules." (With the specific case of giving up red meat—and therefore eating fish—on Fridays during Lent, the origin is murky. It may be related to the view that fish are a different class of animal because God created water creatures on a different day than land creatures or because abstaining from food with blood in it honors Jesus' shedding of blood, which occurred on a Friday.) Many Christians today take a personalized approach and apply fasting to things other than food. Whether it's chocolate, alcohol, reality television, social media, or even sex, Christians often "give up" something for Lent. The key impulse is to refuse some material thing you desire and in this way focus on spiritual things—although, as we'll see below, the reasons humans fast are varied and complex.

For churches that use a lectionary (a common set of Scripture passages assigned for the days of the church year), the emphasis on fasting comes at the start of Lent. The Gospel reading for Ash Wednesday includes Jesus' teaching on fasting from the Sermon on the Mount:

> And whenever you fast, do not look dismal, like the hypocrites, for they disfigure their faces so as to show others that they are fasting. Truly I tell you, they have received their reward. But when you fast, put oil on your head and wash your face, so that your fasting may be seen not by others but by your Father who is in secret; and your Father who sees in secret will reward you. (Matt 6:16-18)

To be sure, Jesus doesn't link fasting to any specific time of the year, and he certainly wasn't talking about Lent. But he does talk about fasting as something his Jewish audience would be familiar with. Although he criticizes how some people conduct themselves while fasting, he doesn't say fasting itself is bad. And since it was Christians who recorded and circulated Jesus' words on fasting, we can presume the practice remained common among early Christians (and this is confirmed by post-biblical sources). Still, Jesus does not offer anything like a program for fasting. His practical advice consists only of directions for how to present oneself while fasting. And his theological insight consists only of a vague reference to receiving a "reward" from your heavenly Father. In this passage, Jesus does not address the *who, what, when, where,* or *why* of fasting.

Take a few minutes to write your thoughts to these questions:

1. What is fasting for?
2. How is fasting best done?
3. If you have fasted during Lent, why did you fast?
4. Have you fasted outside of Lent? Why?

Plainly stated, fasting describes the experience of *denial* of something good or pleasurable. In most cases, we could substitute the word "abstain" and get the same meaning, although fasting generally suggests a temporary experience. Fasts are meant to be broken—eventually. In fact, we break a fast every morning when we eat our first meal of the day—after abstaining from food for eight, ten, or twelve hours—which we call break-fast. But fasting also clearly has religious and spiritual overtones. The Old Testament explicitly mentions fasting forty-seven times and, depending on translation choices, it appears somewhere around seventeen times in the New Testament.[1] As people of the Bible, we should first learn what Scripture has to say about fasting, not to slavishly imitate the practices of biblical characters but to give us some lenses for viewing our own experiences with fasting.

Who: The Human Extent of Fasting

The first question we might ask about fasting in the Bible is: Who fasted? None of the questions we might ask are totally separable from one another. In other words, the *who* often raises the question of *why*, which often hints at the *when* and *where*. But we can keep these issues somewhat discrete by focusing first on what we might call the *human extent* of a particular instance of fasting. In Scripture, fasting may be communal or individual.

[1] Kent D. Berghuis, "Christian Fasting: A Theological Approach" (Ph.D. diss., Trinity Evangelical Divinity School, 2003), 13–14. The Greek New Testament term for fasting can also simply mean "go with out food" or even "hungry," so some debate exists, for instance, about whether Paul's references to hunger in 2 Corinthians 6:5 and 11:27 refer to deliberate fasting.

Communal Fasting

The Old Testament emphasizes the communal nature of relationship with God in a way that modern believers aren't always comfortable with. Beginning with God's promise to Abraham and his descendants in Genesis 12, it is clear that God has a chosen *people*. This is classically expressed in Deuteronomy 7:6-8, where God calls the Israelites "a people holy to the Lord your God" whom he has chosen "out of all the peoples on earth to be his people, his treasured possession." In recent years, it has become fashionable to argue that God freed the Israelites from Egypt because God always sides with the poor and downtrodden.[2] But the Bible is clear: As this passage explains, God liberated the Israelites because he "kept the oath that he swore to your ancestors." God chose this people *as a particular people*, making them holy by that very choice and committing himself to them. As a holy people, God's people thought of blessings and curses, prosperity and adversity, sin and righteousness largely in communal terms. So fasting, whatever it was *for*, was most often a community affair for God's people in the Old Testament.

A prime example of this appears in Ezra 8. Ezra was a priest and scribe (expert on Moses's law) in the fifth century before Christ. About a century prior to Ezra's work, the Jews had been conquered and exiled by the Babylonians. After about four decades (and with the rise of a new regional superpower, Persia), Jews had begun returning

---

[2] "In Israel, God is the Savior par excellence. Beginning with the exodus, God's righteousness is for those who are weak and helpless." James H. Cone, *A Black Theology of Liberation*, Twentieth Anniversary Edition (Maryknoll, NY: Orbis, 1990), 128. See also pp. 4, 104, and Gustavo Gutiérrez, *A Theology of Liberation: History, Politics, and Salvation*, ed. Caridad Inda and John Eagleson (Maryknoll, NY: Orbis, 1973), 155–59.

to Jerusalem. Returning Jews had succeeded in rebuilding the temple in Jerusalem and celebrating holy days. Ezra sensed the need for religious leadership for the reforming community and to swell the numbers of Jews to populate the Holy Land, so he and a sizable contingent of leaders relocated from Babylon to Jerusalem. At the outset of the journey, Ezra decreed a fast for the traveling band. Although not recording specific details of the fast, Ezra explains that in this practice, the people "deny" themselves. The purpose, according to Ezra, was "to seek from [God] a safe journey for ourselves, our children, and all our possessions" (v21). In other words, they were pleading for the welfare of the community. The stakes were high, not only because the travelers were at risk, but because Ezra had boasted to the ruler of the land they were leaving that because God is "gracious to all who seek him" (v22), they would not need military protection on their journey. Securing God's protection was not just a matter of safety of the people, it was also about saving face before the pagan world. So the group fasted, as Ezra ordered, and God brought them safely to Jerusalem. At the core of the entire episode is a communal view of relating to God. As a leader of the Jews, Ezra believed the Jews' return to their homeland was a communal endeavor. If they needed to fast to make it happen, the whole community would fast.

This communal view of fasting even extends in Israel's Scripture to non-Israelites. The book of Jonah recounts how God strangely commanded the prophet Jonah to preach to the inhabitants of the pagan city of Nineveh. Jonah famously resisted the command—probably because his view of Israel being a "chosen people" didn't account for giving pagans a chance to mend their ways. Convinced by a near-death experience (or perhaps even death and resurrection) involving a large fish, Jonah finally brought the message of God's anger to the wicked Ninevites. Specifically, the message was, "Forty days more, and Nineveh shall be overthrown" (3:4). Their response to the prophet's word surprised Jonah. The king of Nineveh first demonstrated his own anguish and remorse by covering himself with sackcloth and sitting in ashes (an early precedent for Ash Wednesday). Then he decreed a fast for the entire city: "No human being or animal, no herd or flock shall taste anything" (v7). Furthermore, Jonah ordered the king, all humans and animals were to call upon God and "turn from their evil ways and from the violence that is in their hands" (v8). All this was in the hopes that God would change his mind and not destroy the city. Again, the community as a whole fasted in an effort to ensure wellbeing of the community.

Recounting the other instances of such communal fasting in the Old Testament would be tedious. The point is clear: When fortunes are necessarily communal in nature, any practice of fasting will also be communal—perhaps even including the livestock! Although this can seem foreign for those accustomed to thinking of spiritual practices in more personal terms, national days of prayer and fasting have been common throughout American history. During the Revolutionary War, Congress annually decreed such observances, the first penned by Thomas Jefferson—certainly no advocate of traditional religion! Specific days of fasting popped up again during war times—undoubtedly those moments in which we feel most acutely that our personal welfare is intimately bound to the fate of the community, that is, the nation. In the thick of the Civil War, Abraham Lincoln appointed April 30, 1863, as "a day of national humiliation, fasting and prayer" to "confess our national sins, and to pray for clemency and forgiveness."[3] Likewise, President Wilson declared "a Day of Public Humiliation, Prayer and Fasting" on May 11, 1918.[4]

Although Christians often individually choose different things to fast *from* during Lent, we can view Lent as a communal fast. We are reminded that the Lenten fast is a communal affair as we hear the words from the prophet Joel that open Ash Wednesday:

> Sanctify a fast,
>   call a solemn assembly.
> Gather the elders
>   and all the inhabitants of the land
> to the house of the Lord your God,
>   and cry out to the Lord.
> Blow the trumpet in Zion;
>   sanctify a fast;
> call a solemn assembly. (Joel 1:14, 2:15)

Beyond being summoned to fast together in Lent, we are communally bound in our fasting practice by the fact that this fast begins and ends for all at the same times (Ash Wednesday, Easter Sunday) and through common symbols, rituals, and words that help facilitate a shared experience (church soup suppers are a great example).

Individual Fasting

Of course, the religion of Scripture—including the Old Testament—is not only a corporate matter. Individuals also engaged in practices

---

[3] https://www.abrahamlincolnonline.org/lincoln/speeches/fast.htm. Accessed June 4, 2023.

[4] https://www.presidency.ucsb.edu/documents/proclamation-1445-decoration-day-1918 . Accessed June 4, 2023.

of fasting that had no direct bearing on the community. Many are familiar with the least flattering episode in the life of King David: his lust, adultery with Bathsheba, and conspiratorial assassination of Bathsheba's husband. A lesser-known detail is that God struck the child Bathsheba bore to David with fatal illness. Despite his grave sin, David turned to God in this horrific circumstance, and fasting was central to his plea. "David pleaded with God for the child. He fasted and spent the nights lying in sackcloth on the ground" (2 Sam 12:16). Not only was this *not* a communal fasting, but David's counselors even urged him to break his fast. A generation earlier, Hannah had a similar experience, although Scripture does not use the word "fast" to describe her conduct. Sorrowful that she had borne no children, "she wept and would not eat," while her boneheaded husband tried to shake her out of her grief-stricken behavior (1 Sam 1:7-8). In extreme circumstances, fasting served as an individual's external, physical manifestation of an inner experience.

> Take a few minutes to write your thoughts to these questions:
>
> 1. How might fasting along with others enrich or enhance the experience?
> 2. If you have fasted during Lent, how did you decide what to fast *from*?

Why: Reasons for Fasting

The Hebrews (aka Israelites, Jews) were not the only people who fasted in ancient times. The practice seems nearly universal, and no single origin of fasting exists. But from the instances of Scripture, we can identify a few major categories of the reasons for fasting, most of which the passages discussed above have already hinted at.

Grief

The most primal motivation for fasting may be grief. This grief may be so deep that it seems akin to death, which is why fasting in the Bible is also often accompanied by covering oneself with ashes—the great symbol of death, as we saw in the previous chapter. In book 19 of Homer's *Iliad*, the warrior hero Achilles refuses to eat in the wake of the death of his beloved friend Patroclus. His fellow soldiers urge him to eat to be prepared for battle, but in the end, it takes an act of covert divine nourishment to put food in Achilles' belly. One possible explanation, then, for fasting, is the symbiotic relationship between emotions and eating. Like Achilles grieving for Patroclus, David weeping for his son, or Hannah despairing of her barrenness, people often reflexively refuse food during times of great anguish. Today we might also recognize this as a symptom of depression. But this also happens in less clinical experiences of grief. Consider the meal that often follows a funeral. The widow who has lost her husband or—perhaps more devastating—the mother who lost her child often needs to be reminded to eat. They literally lose their appetite. As the Psalmist confesses plainly, "My heart is stricken and withered like grass; I am too wasted to eat my bread" (Ps 102:4). Abstaining from food, then, becomes an indicator of immense grief, so that by a sort of reverse logic, refusing food can either signal sorrow to others or perhaps induce the appropriate amount of grief in oneself. (I hasten to add that intense negative emotions can also have the opposite result of overeating or binging. The connections between emotions and food are complex.)

The notions of intentionally displaying or inducing grief may seem odd to our modern Western sensibilities, devoted as we are to hiding and suppressing our anguish—at most revealing it to therapists in very private settings. But ancient cultures seem to have intuited the psychological and social benefits of grieving and engaging in practices (including fasting) that bring grief to full flower. Jesus himself confirmed this basic connection between mourning and fasting when some disciples of John the Baptist questioned Jesus, wondering why they fasted but Jesus' disciples did not. Jesus replies by likening himself to a groom at a wedding. The wedding guests don't mourn while the groom is with them. But, says Jesus, "The days will come when the bridegroom is taken away from them, and then they will fast" (Matt 9:15). Jesus, hinting at his impending death, acknowledges that fasting is appropriate in times of grief. But on the flip side, fasting is not appropriate for times of joy.

Sorrow for Sin

In close connection with mourning, biblical fasting often accompanied sorrow over sins—both personal and communal—and confession of sins to God. A traditional theological term for this is "contrition." The book of Nehemiah opens with the title character, who, like Ezra before him, was part of the exiled Jewish community under Persian rule, getting news that his fellow Jews in Judah were "in great trouble and shame" and that the walls of Jerusalem were in shambles (1:3). Upon hearing these words, Nehemiah records that he "sat down and wept, and mourned for days, fasting and praying before the God of heaven" (1:4). He did not only mourn and fast; he also prayed. And Nehemiah's prayer, in his own words, involved "confessing the sins of the people of Israel, which we have sinned against you." Nehemiah included himself, his family, and his nation in his confession of sin, recognizing the deep offense to God for "failing to keep the commandments, the statutes, and the ordinances that you commanded your servant Moses" (1:6-7). The prophet Daniel follows the same template. Again in the context of the exile to Babylon (although before any Jews had begun to return to the Holy Land), Daniel discerned, based on reading the prophet Jeremiah, that the time of the "devastation of Jerusalem" was coming to a close. This prompted Daniel to turn to God in prayer along with fasting, sackcloth, and ashes. In his prayer, Daniel confessed both God's faithfulness and his people's sin. "We have sinned and done wrong," prayed Daniel, "acted wickedly and rebelled, turning aside from your commandments and ordinances" (Dan 9:5). Interpreting national tragedy and shame as God's wrath, these biblical leaders fasted as an expression of both deep sorrow and admission of guilt.

We could see the stylized prayers of Nehemiah and Daniel as precursors to Christian liturgies of repentance and confession of sin, such as are common during Lent.[5] But in our psychologically

---

[5] The traditional interpretation of the Day of Atonement, which centered on cleansing from sin, includes fasting. Scriptural descriptions of the holy day, (Lev 16:29-30; 23:27-32; Num 29:7-11), however, do not mention fasting explicitly, only that the people are to "humble" or "deny" themselves. See Berghuis, "Christian Fasting," 33.

aware culture, we know that people don't need to say their guilt out loud for it to be real. And as with sorrow more generally, the emotional distress that accompanies guilt often saps one's appetite. A Hollywood cliché is the character in an emotional tailspin after committing some major transgression—say, cheating on a spouse. Often, the guilt-ridden character completely stops taking care of himself. Skipping showers. Home in disarray. And most telling: nothing but condiments and moldy leftovers in the cupboard and refrigerator. Eating is often the last thing on the mind of one who experiences crushing guilt. In this light, the biblical portrayal of fasting alongside contrition makes perfect sense.

Seeking God's Help

Nehemiah's and Daniel's prayers were not only confession of sin. Specifically, Nehemiah prayed for success in his role as cupbearer to the king so that he could advocate for his people, and Daniel prayed for forgiveness, that God would turn his anger away from Jerusalem and instead look upon the city with favor. This points to a third motivation for fasting: seeking God's help or guidance. The standard for this comes from Moses, who ate and drank nothing while on the mountain receiving the Ten Commandments from God (Exod 34:28) and also fasted for forty days while interceding for the Israelites after they made and worshiped a golden calf (Deut 9:18).

By New Testament times, fasting had become typical practice for Jews seeking God's blessing on some important act. For instance, after Paul and Barnabas appointed elders in the churches of Iconium and Antioch, they entrusted them to God "with prayer and fasting"

(Acts 14:23) in much the same way that Paul and Barnabas had themselves been commissioned for evangelistic work (Acts 13:3). Although Scripture doesn't command or testify to it as a regular practice, Christians from very early times fasted in preparation for baptism.[6] Fasting seems to underscore the seriousness of the request to God, and the deprivation of going without food (and possibly drink) may reinforce reliance on God for the ones praying. We should note, however, that Scripture does not give anything like a theology of voluntary fasting. This is especially important to bear in mind when discussing the association of fasting with repentance or asking things of God in prayer, since we must avoid the slightest hint that fasting "adds" anything to the power of prayer or makes God more inclined to grant your request. Rather, God gives out of "his fatherly divine goodness" as Luther so well said in the *Small Catechism* (see Matt 5:45; Acts 15:17) and in response to faith (Mark 9:23; 11:24; Matt 21:22; Jas 1:5-8).

Routine

The final motivation for fasting in the Bible is, for lack of better term, *routine*. Of course, no routine is *only* a routine, so this category can't be neatly separated from the impulses we've already discussed. But this category identifies fasting practices that are observed regularly according to a calendar rather than prompted spontaneously by life experiences. Furthermore, the emphasis in

[6] *Didache* 7. The text is available at https://www.newadvent.org/fathers/0714.htm. Paul did not eat or drink for three days before he was baptized (Acts 9:9-19), but this seems to be an isolated incident related to the trauma of his confrontation with the risen Christ.

routine fasting is that fasting is something of an end in itself, meaning the doing of it is more important than any benefits that might be derived from it or what the practice says about God and how humans relate to God.

The book of Zechariah gives insight into routine fasting. Prompted by a question about the ongoing validity of fasting in the "fifth month" (7:3), the prophet launches into a deeper evaluation of fasting in the Jewish community, mentioning also fasts associated with the fourth, seventh, and tenth months (8:19). Most likely, these ritual fasts were commemorations of trauma in Israel's history, the fifth month and tenth month fasts associated with key events in the Babylonian conquest of Judea and the seventh month fast commemorating the assassination of Gedaliah, a righteous Jewish governor.

We also know from the New Testament that routine fasting was common among Jews of Jesus' day. As the disciples of John the Baptist testified, they and the Pharisees "fast often." The fasting of Pharisees—the religious exemplars of Jesus' day—appears in Jesus' stinging parable of the Pharisee and the Tax Collector. In this memorable story, the two men go to the temple to pray. The Pharisee's prayer sounds like thanksgiving, but it is really religious boasting. He "thanks" God that he is not some wanton sinner like others—specifically "thieves, rogues, adulterers, or even like this tax-collector" (Luke 18:11). Furthermore, he reminds God that he fasts twice a week and gives a tenth of his income. Clearly, one righteous dude! Meanwhile, the tax-collector can't bring himself to look up to heaven but beats his chest, admits his sinfulness, and pleads for God's mercy. According to Jesus, it is this sinner, rather than the pious, fasting, law-abiding Pharisee who leaves the temple "justified" (Luke 18:14). Combined with Jesus' harsh words about how some people fast "to be seen by others," this parable shows Jesus to be generally unimpressed with the way his fellow Jews practiced fasting. But the central matter at this point is that certain Jews seemed to observe a schedule of fasting twice a week.

Interestingly, some early Christians continued the practice of twice-weekly fasting, although they changed the days both to differentiate themselves from Jews who did not confess Jesus as lord and to commemorate specifically Christian events. According to the *Didache*, a document likely written before the close of the first century, Christians should fast on Wednesday and Friday.[7] The justification for the Friday fast, although not explicit in this text, was probably commemoration of Jesus' death. Although less convincing as a primary justification, later sources suggest that the Wednesday fast commemorated Judas's agreement to betray Jesus.[8] Particularly revealing of the early Christian mindset, the specific days of their twice-weekly fast indicates that followers of Jesus do not fast "with the hypocrites," a call-back to Matthew 6:16 referring to non-Christian Jews, who fasted on Monday and Thursday (the "twice a week" of the Pharisee's fast in Luke 18:12).[9]

---

[7] *Didache* 8.

[8] The earliest evidence of this justification comes from the *Apostolic Constitutions* (7.23), a fourth century text. The text is available at https://www.newadvent.org/fathers/07157.htm.

[9] Monday and Thursday are also identified as fast days in Jewish literature from this time or slightly later, justified by the notion that Moses ascended Mount Sinai on a Thursday and descended on a Monday. Berghuis, "Christian Fasting," 61–62, 102–3.

Take a few minutes to write your thoughts to these questions:

1. Have you or someone you know experienced loss of appetite related to grief? Why do you think this is a common reaction?
2. What do you think best describes the motivation for fasting during Lent—sorrow, seeking God's guidance or blessing, or routine?
3. What spiritual practices do you engage in as a matter of *routine*? Does routine strengthen the practice or risk making it less meaningful because one might simply "go through the motions"?

Two Kinds of Fasting

As we've seen, the Bible contains plenty of references and descriptions of fasting. But despite this and the best efforts of early Christian theologians to claim that fasting is a divine commandment, Scripture never commands fasting as a regular ritual or standard prescription for any particular circumstance. Furthermore, the Bible's theology concerning fasting is foggy at best. This means that we are not bound to a divinely ordered procedure or understanding of fasting (as we are with, say, baptism and Holy Communion). As long as we stick to the principles laid out in Scripture, we have a lot of freedom to explore what fasting could mean for us and how it might impact our lives. A helpful guide in this is a sermon that Martin Luther preached on the first Sunday of Lent. The text for the day was Jesus' temptation,

Matthew 4:1-11. In proclaiming Christ's fast, Luther remarked that "the Scriptures present to us two kinds of fasting."

Self-Imposed Fasts

Fasting may be self-chosen, such that one can begin and "end [it] whenever he wills." The key is that such fasting is *voluntary*, meaning that, despite the nearly seventy days of obligatory fasting annually in the Catholic Church of Luther's day (in addition to personal demands to fast as a form of penance), no person or institution has the authority to require a fast for salvation or spiritual well-being (we'll address this more in chapter 5, "Piety").[10] As argued in the Augsburg Confession (the earliest official statement of Lutheran faith, written in 1530), such mandated fasting contradicts the gospel, obscures God's true commands, and unnecessarily lays guilt on people for inevitably failing to abide by all the rules.[11] This may seem like an odd point to make in a book about Lent, a season in which fasting is generally encouraged—sometimes so strongly that it can seem like it *is* necessary. But to resist fasting as *an obligation* is not to refrain from fasting itself. The key is that fasting—like any religious exercise that is not a general commandment from God in Scripture—is always a matter of Christian freedom. You can do it or not do it as you choose, provided you do it (as with all things) in faith. For

---

[10] Eamon Duffy, *The Stripping of the Altars: Traditional Religion in England, 1400-1580* (New Haven: Yale University Press, 1992); K. J. Drake, "Reforming the Fast: Luther, Zwingli, and Calvin on Fasting," *Calvin Theological Journal* 57, no. 2 (November 2022): 217. Luther acknowledged the government's authority to regulate consumption. Drake, 239.

[11] Augsburg Confession, art. 26, Kolb and Wengert, 74–76.

Protestants at least, then, voluntary fasting is what usually comes to mind when discussing the topic, and it encompasses nearly all the biblical examples of fasting we've explored in this chapter. This fasting is an intentional denial of any pleasures or even necessities (for a time), such as Jesus implies when giving his advice to fast "in secret."

One may partake of a self-chosen fast for any of the reasons already mentioned: grief, contrition, seeking divine aid, or routine. Luther focused on how such fasting can be an attempt "to bring the flesh into subjection to the spirit."[12] This extends the notion that fasting can reinforce our dependence on God. This may be what Luther had in mind when in the *Small Catechism* he commends fasting before receiving Holy Communion—while stressing that fasting does not make one worthy of the sacrament. For those who have little or no experience with the practice of fasting, this could be a great entry point: Refrain from eating breakfast the morning before receiving communion during worship. Your physical hunger can remind you of your dependence on God for your daily as well as your spiritual bread. But subjecting the flesh also signals that fasting can be a way to focus our efforts to cut the oxygen supply to our sinful inclinations. As Paul writes, "I punish my body and enslave it, so that after proclaiming to others I myself should not be disqualified" (1 Cor 9:27). And in 1 Timothy 4:8, Paul argues that "bodily discipline is of some value."[13] This

[12] Martin Luther, "First Sunday in Lent," in *Sermons of Martin Luther, Volume 2: Sermons on Gospel Texts for Epiphany, Lent, and Easter*, ed. John Nicholas Lenker (Grand Rapids, MI: Baker Book House, 1986), 135.

[13] This is my patchwork translation. Many translations unnecessarily imply that Paul is denigrating bodily discipline (e.g., "bodily discipline is only of little profit," [NASB]). Much better is ESV: "bodily training is of some value," but "training" rings too much to the modern ear as a reference to working out at the gym.

in no way suggests, however, that fasting is some kind of good work that makes up for your sin or earns God's favor or spiritual points.[14] For starters, fasting does not, on its own, do your neighbor any good. It thus fails the litmus test of God's law, which is summed up as "love your neighbor as yourself" (Rom 13:9). The Augsburg Confession makes this very point—that when rituals such as fasting are required, "the commands of God pertaining to one's calling [are] not praised."[15]

This helps explain the stinging critique of fasting in Isaiah 58. Even though the worshipers made all the right liturgical moves, God lays a harsh accusation: "Look, you serve your own interest on your fast-day, and oppress all your workers" (v3). The "fast" that God asks for is really something different:

> Is not this the fast that I choose:
>   to loose the bonds of injustice,
>   to undo the thongs of the yoke,
> to let the oppressed go free,
>   and to break every yoke?
> Is it not to share your bread with the hungry,
>   and bring the homeless poor into your house;
> when you see the naked, to cover them,
>   and not to hide yourself from your own kin? (vv6-7)

As God speaks through Isaiah, he turns fasting on its head. True fasting is not when you refrain from eating, but when you feed other people. Furthermore, even if fasting from food or other necessities or

[14] The "reward" from the Father that Jesus connects to fasting means simply that God will sustain those who fast rightly.

[15] Augsburg Confession, art. 26, Robert Kolb and Timothy J. Wengert, eds., *The Book of Concord: The Confessions of the Evangelical Lutheran Church* (Minneapolis: Fortress, 2000), 77.

pleasures somehow benefited your neighbor (as may happen when you abstain in order not to cause a weaker believer to stumble, Rom 14), like all human activity it can still do nothing to make you righteous in God's eyes. As Luther elsewhere set the record straight, "Fasting does not justify, but faith in Christ does. If you have this, then you are pleasing to God, whether you fast or not."[16] This is, after all, the point of Jesus' parable of the Pharisee and the Tax Collector. Despite his pious fasting, the Pharisee was not justified before God. Self-chosen fasting can actually be a spiritual snare, since it can lead us to neglect God's law of love for neighbor, inflate our deadly spiritual pride, and open us up to temptation (1 Cor 7:3-5). Furthermore, Luther noted, too much emphasis on self-chosen fasting risks neglecting or despising the earthly blessings God has given us and intends for us to enjoy and receive with thanksgiving.[17]

God-Imposed Fasts

The second type of fasting, according to Luther, is that which "we must bear patiently."[18] In other words, this is not a self-chosen fast but a God-chosen fast. In one sense, God may ordain a fast through a prophet, as he did with Joel, telling the people to "sanctify a fast, call a solemn assembly...and cry out to the Lord" (Joel 1:14). But this was a special circumstance and by no means a perpetual prescription. In the more important sense, a God-chosen fast is that which God imposes upon us, not waiting for us to choose to fast or obey a summons to fast. This is precisely what Jesus experienced in the

[16] LW 29:7, cited in Drake, "Reforming the Fast," 233.

[17] Luther, "First Sunday in Lent," 136.

[18] Luther, 135.

wilderness, where he fasted for forty days and forty nights. He did not choose this course but was driven into it by God's Spirit (Matt 4:1). In this, there is an echo of Moses' fasts on the mountain with God and Elijah's forty days without food (1 Kgs 9:8), in addition to the Israelites wandering in the wilderness deprived of the food and drink they enjoyed in Egypt (Exod 15:22; 16:1-3; Deut 8:2-5). Just so, God often "forces us to fast by the Spirit or by a need we cannot avoid."[19]

Luther urges us to reorient ourselves when it comes to fasting. The emphasis is not on what we do or don't do but on what God does to us. And although we are to receive this fasting willingly, we can be honest that it is not pleasant or pretty. This kind of fasting can involve all sorts of hardships, but it is most apparent in our toughest times. Think about a single mom losing her job, a parent burying a child, or a husband discovering his wife is cheating on him. These are the things that no one chooses for himself, just as Jesus did not choose to go into the wilderness and fast—proven not only by the fact that the Spirit led Jesus into the wilderness but also by the fact that Jesus willingly broke his fast as soon as the angels appeared to serve him a meal (Matt 4:11).[20] In fact, Jesus' experience in the wilderness teaches us three crucial things about God-imposed fasting.

First, God-imposed fasting mostly (if not always) comes upon us through our vocations. The Spirit drove Jesus into his wilderness fast precisely because as messiah, "he learned obedience through what he

[19] Luther, 136. The Augsburg Confession makes a similar distinction in the context of fasting. "For concerning the holy cross they [the Lutheran churches] have always taught that Christians are obliged to suffer, and that this is proper and real, not contrived, mortification." Augsburg Confession, art. 26, Kolb and Wengert, 78.

[20] Luther, 147.

suffered" (Heb 5:8). Our jobs, our core relationships, our key areas of responsibility—these are the sites of both our truest good works (see chapter 5, "Piety") and our deepest suffering. This is true because work and relationships stand under God's curse (Gen 3:16-19) but also because Satan hates it when people are faithful in their vocations; he much prefers people try to avoid these webs of service and accountability. Luther saw that people unwittingly confirm this when they avoid marriage.[21] Vocations like husband and father not only demand much (even all) from us; they also make us supremely vulnerable: dependent upon another for income, responsible to others for wellbeing. One child's chronic disease can bankrupt an entire family. A husband with rapidly progressing Alzheimer's disease can devour a wife's every waking hour and sap all the joy out of a marriage. Unlike in Luther's day when people chose the life of a monk, nun, or priest to avoid such suffering, today people simply increasingly don't get married (or leave a difficult marriage) or have children: U.S. marriage rates have dropped by nearly 60% in the last half-decade.[22] Of course, in most cases, the attempt to avoid suffering in this way is unsuccessful, as single and divorced people consistently experience poorer mental health.[23]

This insight can reframe our experiences of fasting that we have not chosen. To endure loss or deprivation in the midst of your honest work or in the context of family responsibilities is not an indication

---

[21] Luther, 138.

[22] Julissa Cruz, "Marriage: More than a Century of Change" (National Center for Marriage and Family Research), accessed June 13, 2023, https://www.bgsu.edu/content/dam/BGSU/college-of-arts-and-sciences/NCFMR/documents/FP/FP-13-13.pdf.

[23] Jenna Grundström et al., "Associations between Relationship Status and Mental Well-Being in Different Life Phases from Young to Middle Adulthood," *SSM - Population Health* 14 (June 1, 2021): 100774, https://doi.org/10.1016/j.ssmph.2021.100774.

that God has forgotten you or is displeased with you. On the contrary, such experiences are confirmation that you are walking a path God has chosen for you. Jesus endured his God-imposed fast in the wilderness precisely because he was setting out to fulfill his vocation to bring God's kingdom and take our sins upon himself. In the same way, faithfulness to the vocations God has given you may well entail seasons of need. Knowing this does not make these experiences less distressing, but you can be confident that God's Spirit sustains you through it, and the time will come—as it did for Jesus—when God's angels will serve you (Matt 4:11).

Second, fasting that God chooses for us predictably follows the proclamation of God's promise. This is counterintuitive; we would expect that hearing that God favors us and forgives our sins would mean at least that we would receive *no more* suffering than those who have not been chosen by God. But the Gospels are precise about the sequence of events in Jesus' career. At his baptism, Jesus heard the fundamental divine promise: "You are my Son, the Beloved; with you I am well pleased." But Jesus' baptism led directly to his harrowing fast in the wilderness. One could imagine Jesus thinking, *So this is what it means to be God's beloved Son—to be thrust alone into the wilderness to starve?* The same situation faced the Israelites. After God freed them from slavery, he led them into the wilderness, where there was no water or food to be found. *Is this what it means to be God's chosen?*, they thought. But instead of enduring the suffering as Jesus did, they tested God with their complaints (Exod 16-17).

The experience of suffering on the heels of God's promise is ugly not only because it is painful. As Luther reminded his hearers, we experience such God-imposed fasting as the absence of God—just as

Jesus said, "When the bridegroom shall be taken away from them, then they will fast" (Matt 9:15).[24] On top of the suffering is the apparent evidence that God is deserting us or going back on his promise. This is what the stories of the biblical patriarchs (Abraham, Isaac, Jacob, and Joseph) are all about. God made a promise to Abraham that through a son born to him and Sarah in their old age, he would be father of many nations. And then God contradicts the promise by commanding Abraham to kill this son (Gen 22; more on this in the next chapter).[25] God made a promise to Jacob to "do you good." And then God wrestles with Jacob at the Jabbok, nearly crippling him (Gen 32:12, 22-32). God made a promise to Abraham, and restated it to his son and grandsons, that they would possess a land of their own. But then famine (that is, literally God-imposed fasting) repeatedly drives them away from the land of promise (Gen 12:10; 47:1-12).

All this means that it is a dangerous thing to receive God's promise. When I speak with families preparing to baptize a child, I tell them that in baptism the child gains a divine heavenly father and eternal life, but also a sworn enemy, the devil. They need to know what they're in for. What's more, for those who have received God's promise, seasons of loss often bring with them the nagging thought that God has deserted us. And yet, it's worth it. The promise far outweighs the destitution. As Paul says, "I consider that the sufferings of this present time are not worth comparing with the glory about to be revealed to us" (Rom 8:18).

---

[24] Luther, "First Sunday in Lent," 135.

[25] LW 4:95; Steven D. Paulson, *Luther's Outlaw God: Volume 3: Sacraments and God's Attack on the Promise* (Minneapolis: Fortress, 2021), 249.

The final thing Jesus' God-imposed fasting in the wilderness teaches is precisely *what* this fasting accomplishes in us. We'll explore Jesus' temptations in more detail in the next chapter, but at this point we should note that the first temptation goes right for the jugular—or rather, the stomach: "If you are the Son of God, command these stones to become loaves of bread" (Matt 4:3). It is a temptation diabolically engineered for a starving messiah, who certainly had the power to turn stones to bread (for someone who raised the dead, how hard could that be?). Jesus stands firm in the truth that Israel in the wilderness was supposed to learn, "One does not live by bread alone, but by every word that comes from the mouth of God" (v4, Deut 8:3). Jesus' reply to Satan is not just some pious Scripture quotation about food. Jesus knows he is living a new "Israel" moment, faced with precisely the same promise-fasting sequence that showed Israel to be faithless. But the outcome will be different for Jesus.

As Luther preached, to live by God's word means that all that is needed for life is accomplished by God's word. Common sense would say that food is necessary for life. Such a view is even made to sound profound by Maslow's "hierarchy of basic needs," where physiological needs like food, water, shelter, clothing, and sleep must be met before any other needs even surface. But this is a system without God, and thus can conclude, as Maslow did, the exact opposite of Jesus: "It is quite true that man lives by bread alone—when there is no bread."[26] But Scripture teaches that food is actually incidental to life. Remember that in the Garden it was not the inherent qualities

[26] A. H. Maslow, "A Theory of Human Motivation," *Psychological Review* 50, no. 4 (July 1943): 375, https://doi.org/10.1037/h0054346.

of the trees, but God's word attached to them, that made one tree a tree of life and another a tree of death. God's word gives us the nourishment that accompanies eating the bread. In Luther's words, "God sustains us outwardly by bread; But only inwardly he gives that growth and permanency, which the bread cannot give."[27] Similarly, God's word sustains us without bread. Either way, without God's word, we perish.

God imposes fasts on us so that we acknowledge this truth. But God is after more than a mere mental acknowledgement. In our need and deprivation, we are forced to *trust* his word, principally the promise of life through Christ he made to us in baptism. In the final analysis, then, this is what it means to live by "every word that comes from the mouth of God." A God-imposed fast exercises, and thereby strengthens, our faith. As we'll see in the next chapter, God actually tests us in these experiences, both to prove our faith and to increase it. However far you have made it in the life of faith, you have no doubt experienced this. In the words of the great hymn, "when all supports are washed away, he then is all my hope and stay."[28] You may not feel that your faith increases right away, but God plays the long game with these things, and faith works its power quite apart from your feelings.

You might think that this same kind of faith-filled dependence can be accomplished with self-chosen fasting, but here lies the great difference, and thus the reason that God imposes fasts on us. With

---

[27] Luther, "First Sunday in Lent," 141.

[28] "My Hope is Built on Nothing Less," *Evangelical Lutheran Worship*, #596, (Minneapolis: Augsburg Fortress, 2006).

a self-chosen fast, the impulse is always close at hand to trust in the power of your own "spiritual" works, meaning by default that your faith is not placed in God's word alone. Just as "one does not live by bread alone," neither does one live by fasting alone, or any other self-chosen righteousness. In any fasting God imposes on us, we are finding the true source of life.

Concluding Meditation

Lent issues the call to deny ourselves pleasures, comforts, luxuries, and even—temporarily—necessities. Like scenes of fasting in the Bible, such self-chosen fasting may occur alone or with others, may be spontaneous or routine, and may accompany grief, contrition, or pleas for God's help. Such fasting can deepen emotions, reinforce dependence on God, and hold sinful inclinations in check. But it can also be a snare, since we are inclined to trust in our own spiritual exercises. So God imposes fasts on us, ensuring that those who have heard his promises live only by every word that comes from his mouth.

QUESTIONS FOR DISCUSSION:

1. How do you react to the notion that the Holy Spirit drives Jesus—and us—into fasting?

2. Recall a time in your life when God was imposing a fast on you. How did this experience affect your faith? Who spoke God's word to you in the midst of it?

3. How do you feel about your self-imposed fasting (if you do any)? Is it beneficial? Do you sense the temptation to think that you are holy or righteous in God's eyes (be honest)?

4. Of the dimensions of fasting addressed in this chapter (individual, communal, grief, contrition, seeking God's aid, subduing flesh), what would be a useful aspect to explore in your own fasting practice?

• CHAPTER THREE •

TRIAL

I KNOW I'M NOT alone in watching a lot of *Looney Tunes* growing up. Beyond the recurring gags of Wile E. Coyote being undone by his devices to kill Roadrunner and Bugs Bunny outsmarting Elmer Fudd, a common trope in these animated shorts was the appearance of two supernatural beings perched on the shoulders of a character who is contemplating doing something bad. A devil figure sits on one shoulder and an angel on the other, each making his case—the devil encouraging the bad behavior, the angel calling for restraint. As entertaining and silly as this image can be, this is actually how many twentieth-century Americans think of temptation (more of our theology comes from popular media than we would like to think!).

Reckoning with James

In our culture, "temptation" has a somewhat narrow meaning. We think of it as being attracted to something we know is wrong, like lying about a co-worker to get ahead in your career, over-eating when you are already in bad health, or flirting with someone who is married. And like that devil-and-angel scenario, we think of the moment of temptation as a moment of decision between good and evil. But in the Bible, temptation covers more ground—it's not just an invitation or enticement to sin but also includes trials, tests, tribulations, and challenges.[1] So, as we move through this chapter, I'll use terms like temptation, trial, and test interchangeably. Buckle up, because this might challenge how you've thought about temptation.

When searching for biblical wisdom on temptation, many turn to James 1:13-15:

> No one, when tempted, should say, "I am being tempted by God"; for God cannot be tempted by evil and he himself tempts no one. But one is tempted by one's own desire, being lured and enticed by it; then, when that desire has conceived, it gives birth to sin, and that sin, when it is fully grown, gives birth to death.

James means well. He wants to reassure us. He wants us to be confident in God's goodness—that is, that God is both morally good and wants good things for us. For James, this all adds up to the conclusion that God doesn't tempt us. In James' view, the devil teams up with our own desires to lead us down the path of sin. The image of the angel and the devil on each shoulder might fit this perspective pretty well.

---

[1] The Greek word is πειράζω *peirazo*, meaning to test, put to the test, try; from root word for "to pierce."

James' approach sounds simple enough. But it gets complicated when we look at other parts of the Bible. James claims to be a follower of Christ, and he presumably wrote for Christians, but as Martin Luther pointed out in his introduction to this letter, it never once says anything about Jesus' suffering, death, resurrection, or "the Spirit of Christ."[2] In fact, James has a blind spot about Jesus' work in general, and this is apparent in his views on temptation. James says that "God cannot be tempted by evil," but we know that Jesus—who is God—was tempted by evil in the wilderness. (Beyond that, the preacher in Hebrews says that Jesus "in every respect has been tempted as we are" [4:15 ESV]). How do we reconcile that?

What is even more consequential for believers is James' assertion that God "tempts no one." Unless one defines temptation in the narrowest way possible—as someone or something directly enticing a person to sin—James' claim simply doesn't hold water. God cannot be absolved of any involvement in a person's trials and temptations. Scripture tells us that God does all things (Isa 45). The way Luther expressed it was that God causes all things to happen by necessity, although he used the word "necessity" with reluctance because it suggests that God forces or compels humans to behave against their will.[3] Even when we rightly point the finger at the devil for his role in our temptations, we recognize that God's almightyness means that God "moves and acts also in Satan and ungodly man."[4]

---

[2] LW 35:396.

[3] *The Bondage of the Will*, LW 33:39, 42. God's omnipotence is the heart of this great work from Luther.

[4] LW 33:176.

Look at Job's story, for example. Job didn't know why he was suffering, but the first two chapters of the book give us a glimpse behind the scenes. We see God and Satan nearly negotiating over what will happen to Job. God is clearly in charge, and Satan—who directly inflicted Job's sorrows—can't do anything to Job without God's permission. Although Job struggled to understand the reason for his suffering, he correctly saw that God was ultimately responsible. When God finally answers Job's complaints, God doesn't defend himself by blaming Satan for Job's misfortune. Rather, God's answer to Job is that God is God and Job is not (Job 40-41).

This same view shows up in the apostle Paul's testimony of his thrilling spiritual experiences followed by grievous trials. In a tongue-in-cheek defense of his authority as an apostle, he "boasted" to the Corinthians about his "visions and revelations," including being "caught up into paradise" (2 Cor 12:1, 4). Paul recognized, however, the spiritual danger lurking in such ecstatic experiences—namely pride. So, "to keep me from being conceited" (ESV), Paul testified, "a thorn was given to me in the flesh." God was the one who sent this thorn. And this thorn was none other than "a messenger of Satan," whose job was to torment the apostle (2 Cor 12:7). Similar to the way God authorized Satan to torture Job, God employed a satanic minion to test Paul.

This unsettling conspiracy between God and the devil is also at the core of Jesus' temptation in the wilderness. As we saw in the previous chapter, Jesus did not *choose* to go to the wilderness and do without food and water for forty days. He was driven there. This fast was forced upon him. But it was not the devil who drove him into this place of temptation, it was God the Spirit (Mark 1:12; Matt 4:1; Luke 4:1). Of course, Satan has a starring role in this drama, which we will explore in more detail below. But first, we must consider the quintessential trial of the Old Testament, one in which Satan makes no overt appearance at all.

Without any rational reason, God chose Abraham. God made promises to Abraham that had no conditions attached. When the promises seemed threatened, God reiterated them. Abraham believed God, and God reckoned him righteous for it (Gen 15:6). As the apostle Paul explained, in Abraham's story, we have the gospel in microcosm: God promises, we believe apart from any verifying evidence, and God considers us righteous by faith apart from any works (Rom 5). But to state it this simply risks obscuring the most profound experiences in the life of the believer—specifically that of God testing us.

Such trials involve God actually contradicting his promise. God had indeed promised that Abraham's son Isaac (himself the result of God's promise) would be the offspring through which his numerous descendants would be reckoned (Gen 17:19; 21:12). But then "God did tempt Abraham" (Gen 22:1, KJV). God did this by commanding Abraham to murder Isaac. Thus God changed from being Abraham's best friend to being a tyrant. Not only did this seem to go against the concern for life that God had established throughout the preceding chapters of Genesis, but this was a direct contradiction of God's promise regarding Isaac. How could it be that God both established a covenant with Isaac and his offspring and commanded that Isaac be killed before he sires any children? Such trials are not to be comprehended but endured. And Luther was convinced that any attempt, like James', to relieve God of responsibility for temptation was to treat the matter "coldly," as he told his students in a lecture on Genesis.[5] Later in this chapter, we'll see what a "hot" handling of temptation means for distinguishing between God and Satan and confessing what God aims to accomplish by testing us.

Lead Us Not into Temptation

As if pondering God's role in temptation and trial were not disturbing enough, we must also bear in mind that Jesus taught us to pray against temptation. As the Lord's Prayer—given to us by Jesus himself—says, "Lead us not into temptation" (Matt 6:13; Luke 11:4). This is not merely Jesus' suggestion; we are commanded to pray this. And the threat of trial we are to pray against is not just hypothetical or theoretical. "Watch and pray that you may not enter into temptation," Jesus told his disciples in the critical moments before he was arrested, when it was becoming an increasingly dangerous prospect to be associated with this trouble-making rabbi. "The spirit indeed is willing, but the flesh is weak" (Mark 14:38). If, as we noted above, God is somehow involved in our temptations, does that mean we are praying *against* God when we ask him not to lead us into temptation? It's a tough question, but it's the kind of question that honestly addresses the complexity of our experience of temptation.

On one hand, we can resolve this tension by appealing to human weaknesses and limitations. Although trials may come from God's hand, we recognize that they are actual threats; the danger is

[5] LW 4:92.

real—the danger of falling into sin, that is. Whether we're talking about God or Satan as the cause of temptation (more on that later in this chapter), we face powers that are greater than ourselves. Jesus acknowledges this and warns us to pray against temptation so that we might not fall into sin.

But on the other hand, when we pray that God would not lead us *into* temptation, we are talking about more than a situation or circumstance that might present an attractive opportunity for sin. Life is full of trials. Being God's chosen (as you are through baptism) does not dissolve or eliminate the trials that are part of life. In fact, it may increase them. As Scripture says, "Like a roaring lion your adversary the devil prowls around, looking for someone to devour" (1 Pet 5:8). Jesus' command to pray, "lead us not into temptation," is not a sideways promise of peace and security, as if we could attain a trial-free life if we just kept praying these words. We can no more stop temptations than we can keep the birds from flying over our heads.[6] Anyone who drives regularly in the traffic of a large, congested city knows that temptation and trial are not just daily but sometimes predictable occurrences. Like a former nun who recently revealed that she encountered emotional abuse and petty jealousies in her monastery, Christians are sometimes surprised that trial and temptation follow them even when they make great effort to avoid them.[7] We are put on trial both by being harassed by outside forces that cause us suffering and aggravation and our inner impulses

[6] LW 42:73.

[7] "A Former Nun on Why She 'Cloistered' and Later Ran Away," Fresh Air, March 20, 2024, https://www.npr.org/2024/03/20/1197964056/cloistered.

toward unlawful self-gratification. Rather, our prayer here is that God would protect us amid trials and temptations. As Luther put it in a sermon on the Lord's Prayer,

> Therefore we do not say [in this prayer], "Spare us the trial," but, "Do not lead us into it." It is as if we were to say, "We are surrounded on all sides by trials and cannot avoid them; however, dear Father, help us so that we do not fall prey to them and yield to them, and thus be overcome and vanquished.[8]

It would be naïve to think that we could avoid temptation altogether. But it's not naïve to pray that God would not let us be overcome by it. There is a difference between experiencing temptation or trial and falling into (or better, *under*) the power or dominion of temptation. When we pray, "lead us not into temptation," we're asking God to keep us from falling prey to temptation, not necessarily being spared from it. For a concise description of this, one is hard-pressed to improve on Luther's explanation of this part of the Lord's Prayer in the *Small Catechism*, written as a simple guide for teaching children the basics of the faith:

> ...we ask in this prayer that God would preserve and keep us, so that the devil, the world, and our flesh may not deceive or mislead us into false belief, despair, and other great shame and vice, and that, although we may be tempted [*angefochten*] by them, we may finally prevail and gain the victory.[9]

---

[8] LW 42:71.

[9] Robert Kolb and Timothy J. Wengert, eds., *The Book of Concord: The Confessions of the Evangelical Lutheran Church* (Minneapolis: Fortress, 2000), 358. I have used the word "tempted" where the translators have "attacked," as throughout Luther's

One can sense in Luther's explanation that what he's concerned with are not the typical temptations "of the flesh," like stealing or fornicating. Although such things are and remain sin—especially since they do real harm to our neighbors—they are not the Christian's worst enemy. What Christians should really be concerned with—and what all other sins are ultimately driving towards—is "false belief" and "despair." This is nowhere clearer in Scripture than in the scene of Jesus' temptation.

Jesus' Temptations and Ours

As we already noted, Jesus was tempted in every way that we are. That's right, *every* way—including the temptations of jealousy, greed, and lust we muddle through on a daily basis. As uncomfortable as that thought is, it is necessary, because we believe that Jesus was truly, fully human. Of course, Jesus was also, paradoxically, truly, fully God. This is why, despite his temptations, he did not sin. This means Jesus faced temptation throughout his life, not only at the end of his forty-day fast in the wilderness. Nevertheless, there is much all Christians can learn from Jesus' wilderness temptation. This must be why the Gospels of Matthew, Mark, and Luke all describe it, with Matthew and Luke giving significant details. The Holy Spirit wants us to note not only that Jesus was truly tempted (and resisted sin) but *how* Jesus was tempted and *how* he responded.

works, the root word *Anfechtung* is often translated as "temptation." See, for example, this passage in Theodore Gerhardt Tappert, trans., *The Book of Concord: The Confessions of the Evangelical Lutheran Church* (Philadelphia: Fortress Press, 1959), 347–48.

Read Matthew 3:13-4:11 and write your thoughts to these questions:

1. What was the setting for Jesus' temptation?
2. What do you think Jesus was thinking before and during his temptation?
3. How would you categorize the types of temptations Jesus experienced? What does Jesus' response teach us?
4. What have been the most difficult "wilderness" moments of your life?

The first thing to note about Jesus' temptation is what happened immediately *before* it. As we noted in the previous chapter, Jesus comes to his great trial in the wilderness on the heels of his baptism. Of all the encouraging and delightful events in Jesus' life—healing the blind, raising the dead, feeding five thousand—I have to believe that nothing holds a candle to coming out of the muddy Jordan River, watching the sky split open and the Holy Spirit descend like a dove and hearing the most gracious words God can utter: "This is my Son, the beloved, with whom I am well pleased" (Matt 3:17). Yet as great as this is, it only seems to make the next episode in Jesus' life that much bleaker. Although in earthly affairs, being the son of a king means a life of power, ease, and delights, apparently, being God's beloved Son means weakness, starvation, and tribulation. How odd it is, as Luther remarked in his sermon on Jesus' temptation, "that one should lay hold of heaven and ever be in want."[10] The lesson for Christians is clear, for our baptism unites us to Jesus' death and life. We can certainly expect trials and temptation to follow closely behind God's gracious promises.

The second takeaway from the scene of Jesus' temptation is the state he was in. Jesus endured nearly everything—physical and emotional—that typically weakens a person, thus making him particularly ripe for temptation. Jesus was alone. Not only did he not have any human companions in the wilderness, but it seems like God has also abandoned him. The devil has a lot to say to Jesus in the wilderness, but God has gone silent, after speaking such life-giving words in Jesus' baptism. It's hard not to see this as a dress rehearsal for God's ultimate abandonment of Jesus on the cross, when Jesus himself cries out "My God, my God, why have you forsaken me?" (Matt 27:46). And let's not forget the hunger. As the old candy bar commercial used to say, "you're not you when you're hungry." Of course, in Jesus' case, this goes beyond feeling "hangry." We are dealing with deadly levels of nutrition deprivation, a state sure to affect his ability to think clearly. Again, we should take the hint: Grave temptation is likely to come upon us when we are in a vulnerable state—lacking basic needs, without the support of others, or otherwise feeling abandoned by God. As Luther rhetorically asked in his sermon on Jesus' temptations, "What kind of temptation would it be, if we were not forsaken, and stood not alone?"[11]

---

[10] Martin Luther, "First Sunday in Lent," in *Sermons of Martin Luther, Volume 2: Sermons on Gospel Texts for Epiphany, Lent, and Easter*, ed. John Nicholas Lenker (Grand Rapids, MI: Baker Book House, 1986), 146.

[11] Luther, 137.

We can also learn about how temptation works by exploring the three incidents of temptation the devil threw at Jesus. Each of these temptations works on multiple levels. First is the specific thing that the devil tries to goad Jesus into doing. Second is the broader category of temptation that each temptation represents. Finally, we note the deeper, spiritual stakes at play.

Matthew and Luke agree that the devil's first attempt zeroed in on food. "If you are the Son of God, command these stones to become loaves of bread" (Matt 4:3; see Luke 4:3). Given Jesus' hunger, this is a no-brainer tactic. The devil simply wants Jesus to use his powers to relieve himself of his hunger. This temptation touches on the broader category of bodily desires with which we all, having bodies with cares, are experts in. We are particularly susceptible to this temptation during times of poverty and lack. Of course, tending to our bodily cares is not itself sinful. Jesus teaches us to pray that God would give us bread (Matt 6:11), and he spent a good deal of his ministry demonstrating that eating and drinking do not make one less holy or righteous. In some cases, satisfying hunger is even more important than sticking to strict rules about what one should or shouldn't do on the Sabbath (Mark 2:23-28). Such bodily cares, however, are warped into temptation to sin when we desire food for unhealthy reasons and even when we reject food in a distorted attempt to perfect our bodies. Consider your own relationship to food. Do you find yourself binging, putting away a whole bag of potato chips or bucket of ice cream, using the quick rush of fat and sugar as a compensation for emotional pain? Do you starve yourself, depriving your body of basic nutrition to attain an unrealistic physical ideal? The glutton as well as the anorectic faces temptations in this arena.

The deeper spiritual issue is trusting that God will care for and provide for us, as Jesus' response shows. Should Jesus trust that bread would keep him alive or trust that God's word is the ultimate source of life, bread or no bread? As Jesus knows from experience and has Scripture to back him up, we do not live by bread alone but by God's word. Jesus may have been hungry, but he was still (miraculously) alive after forty days without food or water. He plainly knew that God keeps alive anyone he chooses only by the power of his word. To turn stones to bread and eat would only be gratifying a bodily desire, as Jesus knew it was not necessary for his life; he knew that whatever powers and privileges he had as God's Son, they were not given so that he could satisfy his hunger or other appetites.

But even without being miraculously sustained through hunger as Jesus was, we who have heard God's word of promise know that this word is the ultimate source of life. We cannot trust in food for life. The temptation is reminiscent of the failure of the Israelites in the wilderness who gathered more than one day's supply of manna and quail—it rotted (Exod 16:19-21). Similarly, the fool in Jesus' parable thought that he could rest easy by storing up his crops—but he can't stop death from coming by other means (Luke 12:13-21). Jesus' guidance in the Lord's Prayer to pray for bread can be translated as "give us today the bread we need." This is a call to trust not in the bread but our Heavenly Father who gives it, which is another way of saying, "Do not store up for yourselves treasures on earth...but store up for yourselves treasures in heaven" (Matt 6:19, 20). Even when we have food at hand, God must still give life by that bread; it does not give life by itself—in fact, food poisoning can kill as well as starvation!

Following the order of Luke's Gospel, the second temptation dangled before Jesus is the "glory" and "authority" of "all the kingdoms of the world" in exchange for worshiping the devil (Luke 4:6-7; see Matt 4:8-9). This particular temptation has reverberated in popular imagination as the Faustian bargain, revived in legends of various blues musicians selling their souls to the devil in exchange for extraordinary musical talent. This temptation belongs to the category of earthly power. Like bodily cares, earthly power in itself is not evil. If the first temptation regarding bodily cares is primarily "temptation of misfortune," this is "temptation of prosperity."[12] It rears its head when we get a taste of wealth, power, and feelings of importance. These things have a way of breeding insanity, as one never seems satisfied with one's lot. Land a great job, and soon you're wondering why you haven't been promoted. Buy a beautiful house, and it doesn't take long before you wish you had your neighbor's garage or front porch. Get appointed to a position of authority on a volunteer project, and before you know it, you're scheming to cut others out of the decision-making process.

The flip side of this temptation, pointing to a real spiritual problem, is when we bring these feelings of entitlement to God's doorstep. If we begin to expect or think we deserve more than God grants us, we're liable to make either of two mistakes. First, our view of how God cares and provides for us is tainted so that we start to think God needs to give into our demands to prove his existence or care. Luther referred to these as people who do "not believe further than their honor and power extend."[13] This is essentially the fair-weather believer, happy to

[12] Luther, 145.

[13] Luther, 145.

pray and give thanks to God so long as he gets what he wants, but bitter and negligent of God when the gravy train stops running. Such an attitude is easier to fall into than you might think. You probably know somebody who has drifted away from the faith because God failed to answer some prayer or spare some tragedy. This person essentially holds faith hostage, betting that by doing so, God will give in.

The second mistake that comes along with feeling entitled to honor or power is that we are increasingly likely to do stupid things to get what we think we are owed. We'll step over others in the scramble to the top. We'll rationalize cheating or stealing. The choice is rarely as pointed as "worship the devil in exchange for earthly power," but those who compromise their principles for a more powerful job or betray a loved one for a cash windfall are doing nearly the same thing. Although Jesus responds directly to the terms of the offer the devil puts forward ("worship me"), his reply provides guidance for us in all our temptations regarding earthly power. Any violation of God's law in pursuit of some power or possession reveals that you have made that thing your idol. By your actions you declare that the *thing* is more valuable to you than God. So it is always appropriate to respond to the temptation for *more* with Jesus' words "worship the Lord your God, and serve only him" (Luke 4:8; Matt 4:10).

The final temptation is, "If you are the Son of God, throw yourself down [from the pinnacle of the Temple]" (Luke 4:9; Matt 4:6). Luther noted that we should see this as the tempter's last-ditch effort: When temptations of bodily cares and amassing power don't do the trick, the devil will take a counterintuitive approach. After all, on the surface, this doesn't seem to be a very appealing temptation—at least not in the way that meeting physical needs or accruing earthly power scratch an obvious human itch. (We leave aside for now the very real temptation, rooted in despair, that some have to end their lives.) As Jesus notes, the devil is tempting Jesus to tempt God, testing him to test God (Luke 4:12; Matt 4:7). It is a sort of temptation hall-of-mirrors. And in that sense, this temptation deals with what we could call "hyper-spirituality." The false premise is that, as God's beloved children, God will protect us or bless us in whatever situation we find ourselves. This seems quite spiritual. After all, don't we have just this promise from God, "He will command his angels concerning you, to protect you" (Luke 4:10; see Matt 4:6; Psalm 91:11-12)?

The problem is, though, that many of the situations we might put ourselves in are not God's explicit will. We create or imagine situations in which we would need God's rescue or special protection, putting God on the hook for saving us from our recklessness. This is a temptation that is especially acute for those who are particularly pious, religious, and spiritual. Wanting to seem like superstars of godliness, they may put themselves in a compromised and vulnerable position for no other reason than to demonstrate their own holiness (more on this in chapter five, "Piety"). Or, they may chase after certain self-chosen religious works, thinking that, by doing these things, they gain some special status before God. Such people with their spiritual feats may seem very impressive to us, but all such cases will be disappointed to learn that God does not offer protection or blessing in these circumstances.

The central matter, as Luther saw, is that God's promise of safety in Psalm 91 deals specifically with vocations. We should carefully note just how sly the devil is when he quotes Scripture. He selectively omits the phrase "in all your ways" when he refers to the promise of angelic protection. As Luther preached, "the protection of angels does not reach farther, according to the command of God, than the ways in which God has commanded us to walk."[14] To expect God's protection when we self-select special works without God's command or approval, we are only testing God, trying to hold him responsible for what he has not promised. But when we face danger as we live in vocations God has chosen for us and approved—especially those core "estates" like family, government, and church—we should certainly expect God's protection, which may come in the form of vindication after an injury. In Jesus' case, his vocation was not to die falling off the Temple but on the cross for our sins.

> Take a few minutes to write your thoughts to these questions:
>
> 1. What category of temptation do you experience most (bodily cares, earthly power, hyper-spirituality)?
> 2. What do you do when you face temptation?
> 3. How do you explain the difference between temptation and sin? (Or stated another way, how do you know if a temptation has crossed the line into sin?)

Identifying the Tempter

As we've seen, both God and the devil are involved in temptation. And as James rightly notes, these are not the only actors. Our own desires are also at play. Here we're not talking about desires that are part of the

[14] Luther, 143.

original design for humans but those that are warped by the world, as 1 John 2:16 describes it: "all that is in the world—the desire of the flesh, the desire of the eyes, the pride in riches." For this reason, we often describe the enemies of faith and righteousness as the devil, the world, and our flesh.[15] But when we are in the grip of temptation, we can't help but want a more precise answer to the question, "who is tempting me?"

The plain truth, though, is that God and Satan are not so easily disentangled in our actual experience. In a life where the devil quotes Scripture and God contradicts it, one can't be too sure which supernatural being on your shoulder whispering into your ear is an angel and which one is a devil. The quest to identify particular (or particular kinds) of temptation with either God or Satan is a fool's errand. What is more important is to distinguish between what God wants and what Satan wants from your temptation. In short, the devil tests you to destroy your faith, while God tests you to strengthen your faith.

Let's begin with the devil, because for Christians trials never *end* with the devil. We might want to associate Satan with baser, physical temptations, like Jesus' temptations of bodily cares and earthly power. This is certainly true; the devil wants us to sin by breaking God's laws against coveting, stealing, adultery, killing, and so on. We aim to express this with our narrow modern use of the term "temptation." But it's not so much a matter of what the temptation looks like on the surface as what the hoped-for result is. Unlike God, Satan *wants* you to sin by giving into your evil desires.[16] But even

---

[15] See, for instance, the *Small Catechism*, third and sixth petitions of the Lord's Prayer, Kolb and Wengert, *Book of Concord*, 357, 358.

[16] Luther's German had a similar distinction that he usually followed. *Anfechtung* is the broader category of assaults on our faith. *Versuchung* is a subcategory of trial

these are not Satan's ultimate concerns. If the devil succeeds in any such temptations of the flesh, he is not satisfied with a job well done. He is driving at a deeper spiritual temptation. The devil knows that dealing with such sins are the bread and butter of the church. As we'll explore further in the next chapter, Jesus came not to call the righteous but sinners to repentance. And the church has the power to forgive the sins of any (John 20:23). Although Christians do not welcome or downplay sins of this sort, we are (or should be) experts in dealing with them—through public and private absolution, hearing God's preached word of forgiveness, receiving Christ's blood for the forgiveness of sins. Scripture advises us to be forthright about our need in this matter:

> If we say that we have no sin, we deceive ourselves, and the truth is not in us. If we confess our sins, he who is faithful and just will forgive us our sins and cleanse us from all unrighteousness. (1 John 1:8-9)

I pray this is true in your own experience. You have sinned. You are guilty, but you know where to go with your guilt. And the church, in offering forgiveness, delivers God's faithfulness to you, setting you back right with God. In other words, because of the gift of repentance

---

that refers to being enticed or seduced to sin. But Luther saw the same problem that we have—that Scripture uses only the broader term, leaving it up to context to determine if "enticement to sin" is the intended meaning. This is the reason Luther wished that the common German translation of the sixth petition of the Lord's Prayer read "lead us not into trials (*Anfechtungen*)" rather than "lead us not into temptation (*Versuchung*)." Such a translation, in Luther's reasoning, would be more inclusive, and thus more accurate. LW 42:71. The LW editors err in saying that the word translated as "temptation" is *Anfechtung*, when it is really the later word translated as "trial," which Luther wants to add as a clarifier.

(more on this in the next chapter), Satan is never going to get anywhere enticing true Christians into this or that sin of greed, lust, or hatred.

But the devil will use these types of temptations, and any other tool at his disposal, to drive us to the one grave sin of *unbelief*. The reason this sin, in the end, is the only sin that matters, is because faith—the opposite of unbelief—saves us, while, as Jesus says, "the one who does not believe will be condemned" (Mark 16:16). As Luther and the reformers around him noted often, there are basically two routes to unbelief: pride and despair. Pride is thinking that you don't need God's grace because you are, or will be with enough effort, righteous enough to be acceptable to God. Despair is thinking that you are too great a sinner for God to redeem.

One way despair sneaks up on us is through an accumulation of other sins. The devil turns out to be a very good lawyer; in fact, God's law may be his favorite tool for torture. He knows all the wrongs you have committed, and he is happy to remind you. If you keep falling for the devil's snares of greed, lust, hatred, dishonesty, and envy, if you see no improvement in your righteousness day after day and week after week, it's easy to start thinking that maybe you aren't worth saving or that God's Spirit doesn't dwell in you as you thought. Either way, you stop believing that God's grace applies to you.

Another potential on-ramp to despair is the experience of God contradicting his promise. This brings us back to Luther's observations about Abraham's trial in Genesis 22. As theologians Chris Croghan and Sarah Stenson observe, "For Luther, the story of Abraham and the sacrifice of Isaac is not about philosophical propositions or ethical questions but is about having a God and trusting in the promises of this God."[17] When the signs suggest that God has changed his mind about his promise to you—as when God commanded Abraham to kill his promised and beloved child—Satan slithers in where he had not been before. The result is the nagging suspicion that God is revoking his grace because you have failed God in some way. The reasoning becomes: "I have committed some extraordinary sin, with which I have deeply offended God, so that He is withdrawing the promise."[18] This is precisely why the devil begins two of his temptations of Jesus by questioning the promise God had made: "If you are the Son of God..." If God has withdrawn his promise, there is nothing to believe. And if you don't believe, you are condemned, and Satan wins.

> Take a few minutes to write your thoughts to these questions:
>
> 1. How do you handle moments when you feel unworthy of God's grace?
> 2. What do you feel more prone to—pride or despair?

God's purposes in temptation are the opposite of Satan's. In fact, God wants "to make use of this occasion to crush the head of the serpent."[19] Rather than rushing to defend God in these situations by insisting he has nothing to do with temptation, we learn what God is

---

[17] Christopher M. Croghan and Sarah Stenson, "'A Theological "Who", Not a Philosophical "What"': Luther's Exposition of Abraham and the Sacrifice of Isaac," *Neue Zeitschrift Für Systematische Theologie Und Religionsphilosophie* 54, no. 4 (2012): 440, https://doi.org/10.1515/nzsth-2012-0019.

[18] LW 4:92–93.

[19] LW 4:95.

doing to us with what Luther was bold enough to call God's "salutary lie."[20] First, God is holding up a mirror to us. The heart is exceedingly deceitful. Especially in our "#blessed" vaguely Christian culture, we can trick ourselves into thinking we are true believers when in reality we have a relationship of convenience to God. God wants to make known whether your faith is built on his promises or your relatively comfortable and easy life. This is not likely to be apparent until you are faced with true tribulation. This is why you can

> rejoice, even if now for a little while you have had to suffer various trials, so that the genuineness of your faith—being more precious than gold that, though perishable, is tested by fire—may be found to result in praise and glory and honor when Jesus Christ is revealed. (1 Peter 1:6-7)

If you've ever been jolted from a place of comfort and prosperity to a land of loss or grief, this word is for you. Divine trials are like fire showing the authenticity of our faith.

Second, in temptation, God is exercising our faith. Recall Paul's thorn. Despite the apostle's pleas to God for relief, the torment would not end. But this experience reinforced for Paul that believers only always have God's grace to rely on, leading to the faithful confession that when we are weak in ourselves, we are strong in the Lord (2 Cor 12:8-10). When nothing in your experience confirms God's promise, you have only his promise to hold onto. In other words, when God seems to hate you, you must cling that much more to God's promise of grace, forgiveness, and life. In Luther's words, again commenting on Abraham's trial,

---

[20] LW 4:131.

> Wherever we experience the opposite of a promise, we should maintain with assurance that when God shows Himself differently from the way the promise speaks, this is merely a temptation. Therefore we should not allow this staff of the promise to be wrested from our hands.[21]

This is what makes God's testing "fatherly."[22] In hellish circumstances we not only learn whether our faith is in the right thing, but God strengthens our faith. Of course, this is only true if you have a promise to cling to. As Luther never tired of pointing out, this is the purpose of baptism—as it did for Jesus, baptism gives you a promise that is always valid, that always holds you fast. What's more, the deepest trials always involve or suggest death. Baptism, however, is the promise of resurrection. This is how we know that the core of Abraham's faith, which saw him through his great trial, was his belief that God could raise Isaac from the dead (Heb 11:19).[23] Paul was getting at this when he told the Corinthians that "God is faithful...[W]hen you are tempted, [God] will also provide a way out so that you can endure it" (1 Cor 10:13). This is not a challenge to you to find ways to resist temptation; it is a reminder that God is faithful to his promise. By faith in that promise, you have your "way out," a term that could also be read as "end" or "result." Faith makes our blessed end in Christ just as present to us as the trial we now endure.

Whether we call out Satan or God for our trials, when we have God's sure and certain promise, we recognize that even the darkest temptation is, in Luther's words, "the very best sign of God's grace

---

[21] LW 4:94.

[22] LW 4:132.

[23] LW 4:96.

and love for man,"[24] for here God is conforming you to the image of his Son. On the other hand, in such trials, Satan (much against his wishes) becomes for us a "Dr. of Consolation," because his attacks both remind us that we are in Christ (for he does not waste his time with those who already belong to him) and teach us to take refuge in God's word of promise. Thus, you can even boldly thank Satan for making a real theologian of you.[25]

Concluding Meditation

God rules over all. Although he does not want us to sin, he tests us—both directly and indirectly through the devil. Every believer should expect temptations of all kinds, including common temptations of bodily cares, earthly power, and hyper-spirituality. Less common (thank God!) but more deadly are the great trials in which God contradicts his promise—when we hold a promise of life, forgiveness, and righteousness, yet all we sense are death, guilt, and sin. By tempting you, Satan wants to entice you to sin, so that you'll despair of God's grace. But God wants to reveal what your faith is in and strengthen your faith in his promise. By clinging only to God's word of promise in Christ through these temptations, you have victory over the world, the devil, and your sinful flesh.

---

[24] LW 42:184.

[25] "For as soon as God's Word takes root and grows in you, the devil will harry you, and will make a real [theological] doctor of you, and by his assaults will teach you to seek and love God's Word." LW 34:287. In another oft-quoted reflection on the unintended salutary effects of Satan's opposition, Luther said, "I didn't learn my theology all at once. I had to ponder over it ever more deeply, and my spiritual trials were of help to me in this, for one does not learn anything without practice. This is what the spiritualists and sects lack. They don't have the right adversary, the devil. He would teach them well." LW: 54:50. For "Dr. of Consolation," see Heiko Augustinus Oberman, *The Reformation: Roots and Ramifications*, trans. Andrew Colin Gow (London: T & T Clark, 2004), 63–64.

QUESTIONS FOR DISCUSSION:

1. What advice do you (or would you) give to someone who felt like too big a sinner for God to save?

2. What experience in your life comes closest to Abraham's trial?

3. When questioned about overcoming temptation or despair, Luther often advised people to be in the company of other people, especially believers. How has the church been a source of support for you during times of trial?

4. Do you feel that your faith is stronger now than five years ago? Ten years ago? Twenty years ago? If so, what has strengthened your faith?

• CHAPTER FOUR •

TURN

I don't know what I was thinking.

My five-year-old daughter and I walked into the liquor store on a Tuesday afternoon. We only needed a few things, so I decided to grab a hand basket rather than a cart. When my daughter predictably asked if she could carry the basket, I unpredictably said "yes." Now imagine the scenario: a five-year-old girl, brimming with energy, carelessly swinging a hard plastic basket side-to-side as we walked down narrow aisles arrayed with glass bottles of gin, tequila, and wine. It turned out that the problem was not her swinging the basket into the bottles as I feared, but swinging it into my shin, as we stood together, studying the bourbon section. When I let out a yelp, and said her name in a stern voice, her immediate response was an earnest "I'm sorry, daddy." In that moment, I was a proud papa, and I told her I forgave her.

One of the trickiest things about parenting is responding when your child does something that hurts someone else. It could be snatching a toy from a playmate, hitting a sibling, biting another child on the playground, saying something mean to mom, or thoughtlessly swinging a shopping basket into dad's leg bone. Good parents know that "I'm sorry" needs to factor into the reckoning that follows the offense. But they also know that we ask "I'm sorry" to do double duty. On one level, such an expression of remorse is part of our social glue. These two words can rectify a damaged relationship and restore harmony between siblings, playmates, and even casual acquaintances.

But on another level, parents try to foster more than words. The social script of apologizing when you've wronged another person is not an end in itself. And as every parent knows, it can be very difficult to know whether your child is sorry for the pain he's caused or sorry that he got caught. Parents want their child to feel sorry for doing the wrong thing or hurting others. We do not want to be raising children who become like the all-too-common "famous people who have tried to apologize" but seem constitutionally incapable of taking responsibility for their bad behavior.[1] At the very least, feeling sorry makes it more likely that the child will voluntarily apologize, without mom's prompting, "now, what do you say?" But even more deeply, this speaks to what kind of person the child is and is becoming. The feeling of

[1] Elizabeth Spiers, "Opinion | I Have a Question for the Famous People Who Have Tried to Apologize," *The New York Times*, September 22, 2023, sec. Opinion, https://www.nytimes.com/2023/09/22/opinion/famous-people-sorry-apology.html.

sorrow (which is, after all, the root of the word "sorry") for one's bad behavior suggests a well-tuned morality gauge. People with this moral equipment genuinely want to avoid causing harm to others. When they have caused harm, they seek to make things right and restore relationships. Isn't this what every parent wants for her child?

Repentance and Reformation

In the long Christian tradition, the word for genuinely feeling sorrow for your sin is *contrition*. And in many ways, the Reformation that Martin Luther began with the *Ninety-five Theses* in 1517 was a battle over the nature of contrition—how deep regret for sin functions both in the heart and mind of the sinner and in the community of believers. People who know little else about Martin Luther or the Reformation can often tell you that Luther's break with the Catholic Church was over indulgences. But indulgences, which were a way the church offered to reduce the penalties for sin, were just the trigger for a much bigger debate. Everyone agreed that contrition was at the heart of repentance, and that repentance was foundational to Christian life. The problem came, however, with the definitions and details.

Jesus started his ministry with a call for repentance (Mark 1:15; Matt 4:17). According to the Catholic Church of the sixteenth century, this call to repentance was essentially a commandment to perform the sacrament of penance—a highly structured and theologically complex ritual completely overseen by the leaders of the church. As Luther understood Catholic teaching, the sacrament was made up of three parts.[2] This gets a bit technical, but knowing this context helps us understand what enabled Luther to see the value in a biblical alternative. I will keep the details to a minimum.

The first part of penance for the Catholic Church was the feeling of sorrow for sin motivated by love for God. Recognizing, however, that this perfect purity of motives was a high bar, the medieval church determined that in his mercy, God also accepted sorrow for sins motivated by fear of God's wrath. This was basically the theological equivalent of being sorry for getting caught.

The second part of penance was confession. This was admitting out loud one's sins to a priest. In turn, the job of the priest was to express God's pardon. Crucially, only those sins that one confessed could be dealt with. Biblically speaking, absolution, or forgiveness, is a free and complete gift given by God through his representatives on earth (John 20). Unfortunately, the church of the day often hedged on absolution, with the priest who was hearing the confession offering a limp prayer that the one confessing would be forgiven based on the genuineness of contrition and other "merits," rather than totally forgiving the sinner on account of Christ.[3]

In the third part of penance, the one confessing would perform good works that were meant to offset the penalty God would likely

---

[2] For this summary, I've used Timothy J. Wengert, "[The 95 Theses or] Disputation for Clarifying the Power of Indulgences, 1517," in *The Annotated Luther*, ed. Timothy J. Wengert, Hans J. Hillerbrand, and Kirsi I. Stjerna, The Roots of Reform (Minneapolis: Fortress, 2015), 13–22. For Luther's own words, see Martin Luther, "A Sermon on Indulgences and Grace," in *The Annotated Luther*, ed. Timothy J. Wengert, Hans J. Hillerbrand, and Kirsi I. Stjerna, The Roots of Reform (Minneapolis: Fortress, 2015), 60–65.

[3] LW 26:154. Cited in Steven D. Paulson, *Luther for Armchair Theologians* (Louisville, KY: Westminster John Knox, 2004), 80.

impose for one's sins.[4] The term for this was satisfaction, and the priest determined one's exact to-do list of satisfaction, although priests had standard guidance from the church leadership. For light sins, a few extra prayers or acts of kindness might do the trick. The assumption was that most sinners had more sin than they could satisfy in a lifetime, which was why this system required purgatory. Contrary to common thinking, purgatory is not eternity suspended between heaven and hell. Rather, purgatory is a place of *purging* one's leftover penalties for sin. Purgatory basically gave sinners additional opportunities to make satisfaction, in the form of unimaginable suffering for a great length of time. People believed that those who go to purgatory were on their way to heaven.

Satisfaction is technically where indulgences came in, although each step in the system connected to the other steps. The church decided what deeds paid, or satisfied, the penalty of sins.[5] What first caused concern for Luther and others was the way the church used this power to encourage activities that were obviously beneficial to the institutional church, such as fighting on a crusade or giving money for building projects. The church formalized this system with certificates of indulgence. Technically, giving money was the act of satisfaction that reduced one's penalties for sin, and the certificate documented the act. To the untrained eye, it all looked like people were simply buying satisfaction and going home with the certificate

[4] The church had devised a theory that God forgives guilt (what is supposed to happen in absolution) while humans deal with the penalty of sins—that is, God's just, temporal punishment.

[5] A corollary teaching was the "treasury of merits," which held that the church could adjust penalties for sins by applying the surplus merit of saints.

as proof of purchase. Those who were selling indulgences were not priests hearing people confess their sins, determining if people were suitably sorry for their sins, or even praying that God would absolve sinners. They were jumping right over these parts of penance, going straight to the part that promised to reduce people's penalties. Whatever the church officially taught about indulgences, this practice gave people the impression that there was no need for them to feel sorry for their sins, confess their sins, or even hear a priest absolve them; all this was essentially "covered" in the indulgence transaction.[6]

Luther saw that in this situation, repentance had gone completely off the rails. So, the *Ninety-five Theses* began with a big-picture claim about repentance:

> When our Lord and Master Jesus Christ said, "Repent" (Matt 4:17), he willed the entire life of believers to be one of repentance.[7]

This is why the present book seeks to provide a "study for the entire Christian life." Repentance is not a singular pivotal moment of decision or spiritual action. Until the development of evangelical "conversion" preaching (more on that below), indulgences led the way in spreading a false notion of repentance as a deed that one can call "accomplished." We might even say that the beloved season of Lent

---

[6] The instructions for indulgence sellers stated that indulgence was to be granted to everyone who "has the intention of confessing at a suitable time." Hans Joachim Hillerbrand, *The Reformation: A Narrative History Related by Contemporary Observers and Participants* (New York: Harper & Row, 1964), 38. One possessing a letter of indulgence was to be automatically given absolution by his or her local priest, which technically moved the sequence of satisfaction-absolution back to its earlier form.

[7] LW 31:25.

contributes to this misunderstanding. As many churches sing on the last Sunday of Epiphany, leading into Lent:

> Alleluia cannot always
> be our song while here below;
> alleluia our transgressions
> make us for a while forgo;
> for the solemn time is coming
> when our tears for sin shall flow.[8]

If we lean too hard into the idea of Lent as a distinct "season of repentance," we lose one of the great insights of the Reformation. Lent is, rather, the season that should remind us that there is no "season" of repentance.

What's more, the indulgence transaction had the effect, intended or not, of teaching people that contrition and penalties for sin can—and should—be sidestepped. The popularity of buying indulgences suggests that people saw them as a comfortable alternative to the harsher penalties God might deal out to sinners in this life or in purgatory. Luther, however, claimed that a mark of truly feeling sorry for your sins is welcoming the penalties that come as a result.[9] Such a person sees the justice in getting what one deserves while also recognizing that paying penalties doesn't save anyone but rather drives home to us that God takes sin very seriously. Luther was arguing that Christians live their lives constantly under the shadow of the cross. If all of life is repentance, the Christian never skips over or moves beyond all that goes with repentance—namely sorrow for sin and

---

[8] "Alleluia, Songs of Gladness," verse 3, *Evangelical Lutheran Worship* #318, (Minneapolis: Augsburg Fortress, 2006).

[9] LW 31:29.

suffering punishments for sin. Anything less than this is, in Luther's words, "cutting short grace."[10]

Scriptural Foundations

Repentance was the battleground for one of the biggest conflicts in Christian history because everyone knew repentance was central to what being a Christian was all about. In our day, when the concept of guilt sounds old-fashioned and punishment for sin seems incompatible with a loving God, repentance moves to the sidelines in Christian practice. Some churches, for instance, substitute a communal statement of "aspiration" or a "thanksgiving for baptism" for a proper confession of sin, skipping over a pronouncement of forgiveness entirely. But repentance is not so easy to ignore for those who want their Christianity served biblically.

In Mark's Gospel, the first words out of Jesus' mouth involve repentance: "The time is fulfilled, and the kingdom of God has come near; *repent*, and believe in the good news" (1:15; emphasis added). This is both a direct quotation and a summary of Jesus' proclamation throughout his ministry. If, as most Bible scholars think, Mark's Gospel is the earliest of the four Gospels in the New Testament, these words about repentance were likely the first descriptions of Jesus' message that many people in the first century heard. In fact, when Jesus sent out twelve of his disciples for the first Christian missionary trip, Mark tells us that "they went out and proclaimed that all should repent" (Mark 6:12).

---

[10] Wengert, "[The 95 Theses or] Disputation for Clarifying the Power of Indulgences," 21.

> Read Matthew 3:1-12 and write down your responses to these questions:
>
> 1. Why do you think John paired baptism with repentance? How do these experiences reinforce each other?
> 2. What does it mean to "bear fruit worthy of repentance" (v8-10)?
> 3. What do you think is the difference between the baptism of John the Baptist "with water" and the baptism of Jesus "with Holy Spirit and fire" (v11)?
> 4. What moments in your own life have you been confronted with your wrongdoing? How did you respond?

Repentance is also at the center of Jesus' message in Matthew's Gospel (4:17). But Matthew also recognizes that this message tying repentance to the coming of God's kingdom was not a "Jesus original." Jesus was echoing the words of John the Baptist (Matt 3:2). John also urged those who came to him for baptism to "bear fruits worthy of repentance" (3:8). John the Baptist, of course, knew that the kingdom was coming with someone "coming after" him (3:11), while with Jesus, the kingdom arrived.[11] Regardless of the precise timing, the proper response was repentance. For those who failed to repent

[11] Mark's Gospel presents this transition from the "coming" kingdom to the "arrived" kingdom with typical clarity, as Jesus emerges from his baptism (at John's hand) and temptation proclaiming, "the time is fulfilled" (1:15).

after they witnessed his "deeds of power," Jesus pronounced woe and condemnation (11:20-24).

Of all the Gospels, Luke's comes at repentance from the most angles. As in other Gospels, John the Baptist preaches a "baptism of repentance for the forgiveness of sins" (3:3), and Jesus condemns those who do not repent (11:13-15; see also 11:32). When people asked Jesus to comment on recent tragic deaths, Jesus explains that repentance is the way to escape "perishing" (13:1-5). But it is not all doom and gloom. Luke also provides more encouraging accounts of repentance in Jesus' "parables of the lost" in Luke 15. A shepherd who lost one sheep leaves behind ninety-nine to find the stray. A woman who lost a coin searches her house carefully. When the lost item is found, rejoicing ensues, a faint reflection of the joy in heaven over "one sinner who repents" (15:7, 10). As evident in the Parable of the Pharisee and the Tax Collector (18:9-14), the flip side of this coin is that Jesus' message offers nothing for those who are confident about their own righteousness—or in the language of the parables, those who are not "lost." As Jesus testified, "I have not come to call the righteous, but sinners to repentance" (5:32).

After Jesus' earthly ministry came to an end, the apostles continued to emphasize repentance in their preaching. According to Luke, Jesus himself orchestrated this, appearing to the apostles after his resurrection and telling them that "repentance and forgiveness of sins is to be proclaimed in his name to all nations, beginning from Jerusalem" (24:47). In the sequel to Luke's Gospel, the book of Acts, the apostles make good on this charge. On the day of Pentecost, just weeks after Jesus' resurrection, the promised Holy Spirit came upon the disciples, giving them the strange ability to proclaim God's deeds in dozens of languages. When some bystanders joked that they were under the influence of strong drink, Peter launched into a fire-and-brimstone message about the last days, connecting the gift of the Holy Spirit to blood, fire, and portents in the sky. Understandably disturbed, some in the crowd pleaded with Peter, "what should we do?" Peter didn't miss a beat in responding:

> Repent, and be baptized every one of you in the name of Jesus Christ so that your sins may be forgiven; and you will receive the gift of the Holy Spirit. (Acts 2:37-38)

Throughout the book of Acts, this is the refrain. As Paul summarizes his own evangelistic work toward the end of the book,

> First to those in Damascus, then to those in Jerusalem and in all Judea, and then to the Gentiles, I preached that they should repent and turn to God and demonstrate their repentance by their deeds. (26:20)

From the early days of John the Baptist announcing Christ's coming to the end of the work of the apostles, repentance was the cornerstone of all early Christian preaching.

Of course, Christians did not invent the message of repentance. John the Baptist, Jesus, and the apostles were extending a prominent theme of the Old Testament. That is not to say, however, that Israel's Scriptures consistently emphasized repentance. In times before the prophets (that is, in the eras of Abraham, Moses, and judges) a more common response to God's anger over sin was for a holy man to pray on behalf of the sinners. The first such incident in Scripture appears in Genesis 18. Enraged over the sin of Sodom and Gomorrah, God confided in Abraham that he intended to visit the wicked cities.

Sensing that the visit would spell the cities' doom, Abraham pleaded with God repeatedly with a series of questions that all boiled down to one: "will you indeed sweep away the righteous with the wicked?" (v22). Presumably, Abraham hoped God would agree that condemning a righteous person would be a greater offense than sparing the wicked. God confirmed in response to Abraham's appeals that he would indeed spare the cities if he found fifty, forty-five, thirty, twenty, even ten righteous people. Apparently, though, these ten were purely hypothetical, as the destruction of Sodom and Gomorrah in the next chapter suggests.

A second iconic episode of a holy man interceding on behalf of sinners is found in Exodus 32. After having received the Ten Commandments, the Israelites waited at the foot of Mt. Sinai as Moses continued speaking with God. They did not know what their leader was up to, but this much they knew: They had been miraculously delivered from their bondage and slavery in Egypt. They felt they needed a focus for their awe and gratitude and probably their prayers for the perilous journey ahead. So, despite the commandments against worshiping other gods or making an idol, they did what ancient peoples always did, they made an image of the god they believed had granted them good things and hoped would continue providing for them. God responded by telling Moses to see the atrocity of the golden calf for himself, leaving God alone to stew in his wrath and consume the people.

God offered to start over, begin a new chosen people, with Moses. But Moses sensed more was at stake. He pleaded with God on behalf of the people with two tactics. First, he raised questions about God's reputation. If God destroyed his own people whom he had taken such care to free, what would the Egyptians think? (32:10). Second, Moses threw God's promise back in his face:

> Turn from your fierce wrath; change your mind and do not bring disaster on your people. Remember Abraham, Isaac, and Israel, your servants, how you swore to them by your own self, saying to them, "I will multiply your descendants like the stars of heaven, and all this land that I have promised I will give to your descendants, and they shall inherit it forever." (Exod 32:12-13)

Compared to Sodom and Gomorrah, this story has a happier ending. God "changed his mind" and did not destroy the people (v14), although Moses executed his own vengeance and God still sent a plague. Moses was successful where Abraham was not because the Israelites for whom Moses interceded had a promise from God. Moses's plea on behalf of the people was not based on their real or potential righteousness but on God's faithfulness to his promise. But in the cases of both Abraham and Moses, God seems as though he wants to get talked out of his wrath and so invites the intercession of his chosen man in order to repair the rift created by sin.

For many reasons, as God's people entered and inhabited the Promised Land and established government and patterns of worship, the prayers-of-a-holy-man response to sin became less common. Instead, God expected, and the people understood, that sinners must repent. This shift is dramatically posed in Jeremiah 7:16, where God tells the prophet, "As for you, do not pray for this people, do not raise a cry or prayer on their behalf, and do not intercede with me, for I will not hear you" (see also Jer 15:1). A big-picture view of Christian Scripture recognizes here that as the time for Christ's appearing approached, God increasingly stressed the need for repentance. As we saw in the earlier chapter on fasting, repentance was a common response when people sensed God's wrath. A classic example is, ironically, that of the Ninevites, who, despite being Gentiles, recognize the truth in Jonah's reluctant pronouncement of doom. So the pagan king declared,

> All shall turn from their evil ways and from the violence that is in their hands. Who knows? God may relent and change his mind; he may turn from his fierce anger, so that we do not perish. (Jonah 3:8-9)

This story hardly has a developed theology of repentance, but the key elements are present: When they become aware of God's wrath, the sinners "turn" from evil in hopes that God will "turn" from his anger. This double "turning" (or returning) is the essence of repentance.

Not surprisingly, God's people often did not repent when they should have. The prophet Amos voices God's frustration. God was not shy about his displeasure that his people were behaving badly, especially in their abuse of the poor (2:6-8). He gave "lack of bread," withheld rain, destroyed crops with mildew and locusts, and killed Israelites with pestilence and sword (4:6-11). Yet, God laments in a repeated refrain, "you did not return to me." At this point, God implies that the window for returning had closed: "prepare to meet your God, O Israel" (v12). Other times, however, God's call to repentance through the prophets is more direct. Instead of using disaster and tragedy to stir people to repentance, God simply issued the summons to repent. The prophet Joel is a classic example, and this is often recited at the beginning of Lent:

> Yet even now, says the Lord,
> return to me with all your heart,
> with fasting, with weeping, and with mourning;
> rend your hearts and not your clothing.
> Return to the Lord, your God. (Joel 2:12-13)

Not coincidentally, these words come from the same chapter in Joel that Peter recited on Pentecost, before telling the dumbfounded onlookers to repent. Although inspired and commanded directly by Christ to preach repentance, the apostles also mined the rich Old Testament heritage of repentance proclamation.

The Grammar of Repentance

So far, I have not tried to interpret or craft a theory of repentance from the various biblical messages of repentance. The point has been simply to show how important it was. But that is a pretty useless exercise if we don't see how the message of repentance functions in the lives of sinners who experience it. Just as it was a point of controversy between Catholics and Protestants in the sixteenth century, so the issue of repentance has continued to cause consternation to our day.[12] Although we can't solve all the problems, we stand on firmer ground if we become familiar with what I call the grammar of repentance—that is, the way repentance works in the actual statements of those preaching it.

First, repentance falls upon the ears of sinners as a *command*. As Paul preaches at the Areopagus, "While God has overlooked the times of

---

[12] Walter Sundberg, *Worship as Repentance: Lutheran Liturgical Traditions and Catholic Consensus* (Grand Rapids, MI: W.B. Eerdmans, 2012).

human ignorance, now he commands all people everywhere to repent" (Acts 17:30). Two connected truths are relevant here. First, no one may escape the need for repentance. As the book of Acts carefully demonstrates, no category of person is exempt from both God's demands and his promises. No one is sufficiently righteous or equipped with adequate excuses for sin to ignore the call to repentance. Second, this is a personal experience that will involve a sinner. Repentance happens not in some ethereal way by being around Christians or participating in Christian rituals. As important as being part of a community of believers is, repentance does not happen by osmosis. As Paul the preacher expressly says, the call to repentance happens "now," that is, in the very moment when your preacher stands before you with the command. Repentance demands that something change *about you.*

The second aspect of the grammar of repentance is that repentance is a *gift*. Regardless of how the individual sinner is involved, no one can repent simply because they decide to do so. Repentance is not a power inside of you; you cannot choose to repent as you can choose what shoes to wear or what sandwich to order for lunch. Repentance is not a spiritual version of a New Year's resolution. Repentance happens to you when a preacher delivers it to you in the power and by the command of the crucified and risen Christ. As the apostles told Christ's murderers, "God exalted [Jesus] at his right hand as Leader and Savior that he might *give* repentance to Israel and forgiveness of sins" (Acts 5:31; emphasis added).[13] As scary as this thought may be to

[13] This message is specifically for the Israelites. But as Acts carefully elaborates, the Gentiles (non-Jews) are not left out. As Peter reflects on the salvation of Gentiles, "Then God has given even to the Gentiles the repentance that leads to life." (Acts 11:18). Both instances describe repentance as a gift.

those who do not yet have a preacher, sinners can only wait passively for God to bestow the gift of repentance. In no way can we make repentance into some kind of work or accomplishment. As much as we might tell ourselves otherwise, any spiritual achievement—no matter how miniscule we view it compared to God's grace—too easily becomes an excuse for boasting. This is the opposite of the gospel: "For by grace you have been saved through faith, and this is not your own doing; it is the gift of God—not the result of works, so that no one may boast" (Eph 2:8-9). The moment you feel righteous for having repented is the moment you need to repent again.

Readers may recognize in this language of "command" and "gift" the long practice in the church of referring to God's words as *law* and *gospel*. For many, this means carefully distinguishing those places in Scripture where God clearly demands something (law) and when God clearly gives something (gospel). *You shall not bear false witness*: law. *Come to me, all you who are weary and heavy laden, and I will give you rest*: gospel. This is a useful starting point, but it often fails to recognize how statements actually affect those who hear them proclaimed. For instance, one may hear unrelenting law in Jesus' words, "Therefore I tell you, do not worry about your life, what you will eat or what you will drink, or about your body, what you will wear. Is not life more than food, and the body more than clothing?" (Matt 6:25). These words are, after all, spoken in the form of a command (grammarians call it "the imperative"). Jesus seems to be lecturing us about our worrying problem and urging us to do something about it. Perhaps we stop worrying by building gratitude practices into our daily routine, putting our energy into a healthy hobby, or living a simpler life. Either way, it seems like one more task to add to all the other things on your to-do list. But heard another way (that is, with faith given by the Holy Spirit through preaching), these words are pure gospel. Jesus is giving not a command but the gift of not worrying. "Here," Jesus says, "receive 'no worry.'" Identifying the work of law and the work of gospel is not as simple as parsing grammar. Technically, "Stand up, take your mat and walk" is a series of commands, but good luck trying to tell that paralytic Jesus just healed that he heard anything but gospel (John 5:8). With ears of faith, even the command "go, and sin no more" is the gift of a new life lived out from under the burden of sin (John 8:11 KJV). Even the quintessential words of law in the Ten Commandments may convey both command and gift. From one angle, "You shall have no other gods" (Exod 20:3) is God's ultimate, unattainable standard. To ears of faith, however, this is a beautiful pronouncement that our exhausting and self-destructive search for (and construction of) gods comes to an end, because God has decided to be your God, end of story (Exod 20:2).

The End of Repentance

Although we cannot use grammatical gymnastics to escape the personal demand of repentance, gospel preaching recognizes that the end (both in the sense of the conclusion and the purpose) of repentance is faith. In Jesus' own words, "repent, and believe in the good news" (Mark 1:15). This faith receives a gift freely given, creating a life that upholds God's law while living beyond it. At the risk of making this vibrant and unruly experience for believers too neat and tidy, we can identify several steps in this process.

First, the call to repentance calls you to account for your sins. Repentance is necessary because you have disobeyed God's commandments. As the saying goes, the first step in solving a problem is admitting you have one. If you or a loved one have ever had to deal with truly destructive behavior, like addiction, self-harm, or chronic dishonesty, you know the importance of this "reckoning." Confession and sorrow for sin, and even the intention to do better, are necessary. In Psalm 51, King David gives the classical expression of the sinner expressing this contrition.

> Read Psalm 51 and write down your responses to these questions:
>
> 1. What words does David use to describe his wrongdoing? (Feel free to look at multiple translations.) What are the different shades of meaning of each of these words?
> 2. What do you think is the fear underlying David's plea to God?
> 3. What emotions do you detect in the Psalm? Is there a progression through various emotions?
> 4. When you have felt guilty, what other emotions did you feel? Which emotions were helpful? Which emotions were destructive?

This psalm is a standard "penitential psalm" (that is, dealing with repentance) for many reasons. David helpfully admits that the sin weighing on him is specific: "against you [God]...have I sinned" (v4). He forthrightly admits his sin; he does not make excuses, plead ignorance or extenuating circumstances, or try to deflect by arguing that others are just as bad or worse sinners than he. According to tradition, David prayed this prayer after the prophet Nathan justly accused him of adultery and murder (see 2 Sam 12). But David also recognizes that "sin" is a force greater than any particular misdeed—in fact, sin is more than even the sum of one's wrongdoings. "I was born guilty," he admits (v5). This first step of repentance may often be wrung out of us in a general feeling of guilt and hopelessness that the sinner doesn't yet consciously pinpoint to some sinful deed.[14] In everyday speech, these are the people who walk around with a dark cloud hanging over them.

The prayer for mercy takes on a new desperation when we realize—as Job did—that even being blameless according to God's law is not enough to give us a right to stand upright in God's presence. Job learned that repentance is necessary simply because God is God and we are not—and these bare facts force us to try to charge God with wrongdoing or to take his place.[15] Every act of sin we commit is not a pin poking through some innocence bubble that normally surrounds us but an object lesson of who we are at our core. Put another way, every sin is disobedience against the First Commandment ("have no other gods"), which means ultimately a failure to have faith, to trust in God to be your God. We try to step into the perceived God gap, taking upon ourselves the functions of a god. Those who

---

[14] James Arne Nestingen, "Preaching Repentance," *Lutheran Quarterly* 3, no. 3 (1989): 253–54.

[15] The blameless Job repents in Job 42:6. See Gerhard O. Forde, "Absolution: Systematic Considerations," in *The Preached God: Proclamation in Word and Sacrament*, ed. Steven D. Paulson and Mark C. Mattes (Grand Rapids, MI: William B. Eerdmans, 2007), 152–62.

steal demonstrate they do not trust God to provide. Those who puff themselves up by slandering others demonstrate they do not trust God's pronouncement of their own worth. The final thing David's confession teaches us is that we cannot help ourselves. He opens with a profound plea for mercy, and he acknowledges that the only solution to his sinful heart is for God to perform a complete heart transplant (v10).

As necessary as this first step of admitting our sin is, it does not on its own change our situation. Judas—the disciple who betrayed Jesus to death—repented of his treachery, tried to make restitution, and openly confessed his transgression (Matt 27:3-4). Yet the sad fact is that he died condemned in his sin. The first step on its own leads only to despair.[16] If, for instance, I had responded to my daughter's apology in the liquor store by saying, "that's right, you should be sorry," she may rightly wonder if I'm still upset with her to this day. But the next step occurs when God speaks something other than accusation to us. This word is what David prayed for; and he received it from the mouth of his accuser Nathan: "Now the Lord has put away your sin" (2 Sam 12:13). This word is what Judas longed for, but unfortunately, the people he confessed his sin to had no interest in speaking this word. "What is that to us?" they rebuffed Judas. "See to it yourself" (Matt 27:4). In Psalm 51, David uses many illustrations to envision how God gives mercy and a new heart. God may cover his sin like a white-out pen covers a typographical error (vv1, 9). God may put

[16] See Robert Kolb and Timothy J. Wengert, eds., *The Book of Concord: The Confessions of the Evangelical Lutheran Church* (Minneapolis: Fortress, 2000), 313, 501. (Smalcald Articles, III, art. 3; Epitome of the Formula of Concord, V.)

the sinner through the wash (vv2, 7). God may burn sins away like a physician removes a wart (v7). Or, God may simply decide not to see his sins (v9). The dominant way the church has spoken of this is *forgiveness* (or absolution). Another Psalm encapsulates this:

> Then I acknowledged my sin to you,
> and I did not hide my iniquity;
> I said, "I will confess my transgressions to the Lord,"
> and you forgave the guilt of my sin. (Ps 32:5)

A proclamation of forgiveness seems simple. Some consider it *too* simple to encompass the breadth of Christian life—and so emerge the mountains of Christian literature describing what to do *after* receiving God's forgiveness (on bookshelves and Amazon.com, it is called "Christian living"). But that common perspective fails to appreciate the full effects of this simple word. First, before it does anything else, forgiveness confirms the accusation of the law. Most of us have had that experience of offering forgiveness to someone only to be met with anger and resentment ("what did *I* do that needs forgiving?"). Forgiveness often initially comes across as an insult. In fact, sometimes, this is the only way the law's accusation can get through. Only the sick need a physician. Only sinners need forgiveness.

Second, although forgiveness in this sense confirms what the law says, in the end, forgiveness opposes the accusation we hear from God's law. You have sinned, but God does not count your sins against you. Forgiveness eternally silences God's law. This needs to be spoken, because no one can arrive at this conclusion about God on his or her own. Anyone who is honest will admit that our internal dialogue (for instance, as we look in the mirror or analyze our selfies) is bent towards pride or despair—neither of which ends in forgiveness. When the chief priests and elders told Judas to "see to it yourself," they pushed him back into the echo chamber of his own heart, where he heard only the law's accusation. So the great call to repentance in Joel makes two key moves. First, it proclaims God's graciousness in general, "slow to anger and abounding in steadfast love" (Joel 2:13). As true and necessary as this is, sinners lost in the funhouse mirrors of their own sin and despair often cannot apply this general affirmation to their own condition: *but can God really forgive me?* So Joel moves finally to a direct absolution, speaking it in terms of the reversal of God's wrath: "you shall eat plenty and be satisfied" (2:26).

Finally, by silencing the law, forgiveness relentlessly gives what the law could only demand: "I am the Lord your God." Hearing your sins are forgiven means hearing that God has decided to be your God, come hell or high water. And so dies your seemingly endless desire for other gods, along with all the sins that were expressions of this desire. Scripture calls this living by God's Spirit instead of the flesh. Paul summarizes how forgiveness's release from the law ends up being the only way we can uphold the law:

> Christ redeemed us from the curse of the law...in order that in Christ Jesus the blessing of Abraham might come to the Gentiles, so that we might receive the promise of the Spirit through faith...the fruit of the Spirit is love, joy, peace, patience, kindness, generosity, faithfulness, gentleness, and self-control. There is no law against such things. (Gal 3:13-14; 5:22-23)

In the command and gift of repentance, God creates faith, which transforms us from serial offenders of the law to Spirit-filled saints who couldn't break the law if we tried.

The Entire Life

As a teenager, I belonged to a morally rigorous Pentecostal church. We took repentance very seriously. Such morally rigorous evangelical churches may be the only ones that still do take repentance seriously. But repentance was also very carefully confined to two contexts. First was the "altar call."[17] This was preaching aimed at non-Christians, pleading for them to convert to Christ. Anyone familiar with the preaching of a Billy Graham crusade will recognize the tropes and rhetorical moves of this preaching. It was a classic call to repent: Feel sorry for your sins, admit you are a sinner; ask God for forgiveness; determine to sin no more. Layered into this essentially biblical message was more elastic language of "giving your heart to Christ," "asking Jesus into your heart" and "accepting Jesus as your lord and savior." The other realm for repentance was the "rededication" sermon, which was just as common as the altar call. This preaching was for the Christian who had fallen away, usually evidenced by some pattern of blatant sin—what we referred to as "backsliding." The content of the message was much the same, however: Feel sorry for your sins; admit you are a sinner; ask for forgiveness; determine to sin no more. Repentance was for those who were dramatically and visibly estranged from God.

Although American evangelical churches celebrate Luther's posting of the *Ninety-five Theses* and the way the Reformation emphasized justification by faith and the priesthood of believers, they tend to ignore or dismiss the core claim that began the Reformation: The

[17] An altar call is a common practice among evangelical Christians where a preacher invites people to come forward to publicly declare their decision to follow Christ and be led in a prayer marking repentance and conversion.

entire life of the believer is repentance. More content to consider repentance in the realm of crisis moments like conversion and rededication, American Christians (and Christians globally influenced by this evangelicalism) tend not to see repentance as a daily affair. But this is an unfortunate failure to recognize the insidiousness of sin. As Jesus preaches in the Sermon on the Mount, sin's power is such that as soon as you think you have mastered it, it always finds a way to slither back in. No one is righteous simply because he or she hasn't physically killed a person or committed adultery; the one who hates or lusts is just as guilty (Matt 5:22, 28). As we've seen, all such sins are, in the end, emblems of the deeper sin of rejecting God as your God, a constant tendency for all humans born into this world of sin.

Taking the power of sin seriously means recognizing that repentance is not something that occurs in discrete episodes in life but is itself the very way of life for the Christian. Even as we insist that the Christian does (or ought) to grow in holiness, the effect of this is to make the believer more sensitive to his sin, more aware of her own unworthiness and need for sheer grace, as Paul testifies in Romans 7. "I do not do the good I want, but the evil I do not want is what I do" (v19). This does not mean that we throw up our hands and admit defeat but that we confess both the power of sin and the greater power of our lord who delivers us from sin and transforms us. As Paul continues: "Wretched man that I am! Who will rescue me from this body of death? Thanks be to God through Jesus Christ our Lord!" (v24-25).

Repentance is nothing other than the repeated death of the sinner and resurrection of the saint—dreading the wages of sin while clinging to the gift of Jesus Christ. It is living under the cross while claiming life. Baptism is the great symbol of this.[18] Going under the water, we die to sin with Christ; coming out of the water, we rise to righteousness with him (Rom 6:3-4). As baptism is also the original site of forgiveness, repentance is returning to and using baptism to be renewed in forgiveness. Evangelists like Billy Graham spoke often to their unconverted audiences of the need to repent, while those who were converted at such meetings more often spoke of "discipleship" once they were "saved." The gospel, however, unites repentance and discipleship in the daily life of the believer: "If anyone wants to come after me, he must deny himself and take up his cross *daily* and follow me" (Luke 9:23; emphasis added).

Concluding Meditation

We are by nature God's enemies, children of wrath. When this truth becomes real to us, we sense that repentance is our only possible chance for a different outcome. To turn from sin in hope that God will turn from wrath is not just a human fancy but the fundamental Christian sermon, inspired by the Old Testament prophets, refined in the preaching of Christ himself, and continued by his apostles to this day. In this message is both the demand to turn and the gift of forgiveness for those who turn. That gift creates faith, which forever silences God's accusation while bestowing a life in God's Spirit that the law cannot condemn. While sin within continues to war against the Spirit, we return daily to the forgiveness made so vivid and certain in baptism.

[18] See Luther's *Large Catechism*, Kolb and Wengert, 464–67.

QUESTIONS FOR DISCUSSION:

1. What have been the big moments in your life of forgiveness—either you forgiving others or others forgiving you?

2. Do you know anyone who carries sorrow for sin and can't seem to move past it? How might you or someone else speak God's forgiveness to that person?

3. How have the sins that affect you changed over the course of your life? Were there seasons of your life when some sins seemed more prevalent or threatening?

• CHAPTER FIVE •

PIETY

LIKE IT OR NOT, how you behave day-in and day-out says a lot about who you are. We might imagine that we choose our actions from an endless buffet of available options, but in reality, outside forces put great pressure on us to act in certain ways. Think about how you have reacted to the expectations and regulations of your family, school, or workplace. Did you do what you were told, even if you didn't understand it or agree with it? Did you rebel against the rules, trying to make a statement by doing the opposite of what others expected? Whether you give in to these pressures or resist them, these forces largely set the terms for your behavior; and as a consequence, your behavior shows both what you value and the quality of your character.

Consider these two scenarios.

A new, powerful empire takes over a small, close-knit nation with strong religious beliefs. To crush the spirit of the conquered group, secure its hold on its new territory, and enrich its own culture, the empire forces leading men from the conquered nation to serve in the royal palace. The rulers offer these men comfortable lodgings, education in the empire's language and culture, and rich meals from the royal storehouses. A small group of them, however, refuse the food and wine, requesting meals of only vegetables and water so that they might remain pure.

A different empire, cosmopolitan and centuries old, tolerates an ethnic and religious minority in its borders. This outnumbered group gravitates to a few specific regions, but they live in pockets throughout the empire. Wherever they live, they maintain their identity by observing religious practices they believe come straight from their god. Some take this one step further, showing their identity not only by following their god's commands but by observing traditions passed on from their ancestors. One such tradition is the practice of ritually washing one's hands before eating. They accuse anyone who violates this tradition of eating "with defiled hands."

Both of these very real cases demonstrate another aspect of human behavior that leads us to the final theme in our study of the theology of Lent. Religion and morality are always connected to cultural identity. In response to outside forces, people craft and protect their sense of who they are by doing things that set them apart from others. And they often raise the stakes on these behaviors by claiming they either come from God or at least are very pleasing to God. To observe such practices, then, is to remain pure; to neglect them is to defile yourself, to become unclean not just in the eyes of your compatriots but also in the eyes of God. The case of the vegetarians in the royal palace comes from the story of Daniel and his three friends in Daniel 1. And we know of the careful handwashers from the Gospels in the New Testament (Mark 7:1-13; Matt 15:1-20; Luke 11:37-41). In both instances, the Jews, facing the threat of a dominant pagan culture, double down on religious practices that mark them as different from their godless neighbors. What's more, these practices could serve to separate the wheat from the chaff (so to speak) within the Jewish community. In a time when a different pagan empire ruled over God's chosen people, a man named Tobit testified, "All my brothers and the people of my race ate the food of the heathen, but for my part I was careful not to eat the food of the heathen" (Tobit 1:10-11).[1] This is precisely what caused such consternation for the Pharisees who criticized Jesus and his disciples for eating without washing; the Pharisees couldn't square the way Jesus disregarded religious rules with the clear evidence that he was an impressive religious leader.

Most Christians do not share the Pharisees' worries about eating food with impure hands or Daniel's qualms about eating food that was used in the worship of other gods. But the impulse to use particular religious practices to set oneself apart in the eyes of God and other people—and to strengthen bonds of community through such practices—is as strong for Christians as for any other people. In fact, some Christians look precisely to the Old Testament for such identity-marking behavior. Whether it's the Seventh-day Adventists observing Saturday Sabbath or "Hebrew Root" Christians trying

[1] The book of Tobit belongs to a loose collection of texts known as the Apocrypha. Various Christian groups regard different combinations of these texts as Holy Scripture.

to observe Judaism as Jews practiced it in Jesus' day (even wearing garment tassels known as *tzitzit* per Num 15:37-41), Christians looking for practices that would mark them as different from others can find many ideas in the Hebrew Scriptures. More often, though, Christians try to confirm their special status before God and other people through behaviors that arise from their own cultural surroundings or by extreme dedication to common Christian behaviors. The rest of this chapter explores the ways these practices, which I'll refer to as piety and good works, operate in the lives of Christians. First, we'll look at the many ways piety can go wrong. Then I'll show how, despite all these dangers, God gives us clear direction about what true good works are and consistently gets us to do good for others. The chapter closes with the assurance that through faith and by the power of the Holy Spirit, God brings forth from us the works that he sees as good. Throughout, I hope to hammer home the point that when it comes to piety in the Christian life, it is best if we trust God rather than try to take matters into our own hands.

> Take a moment to write down your responses to these questions (and be honest with yourself!):
>
> 1. What good do you do that you hope <u>other people</u> notice?
> 2. What good do you do that you hope <u>God</u> notices?
> 3. What good deeds or habits do you wish you were better at?

Toxic Piety

Everyone agrees that Christians should do good works. Just as Lent focuses us on the meaning of repentance, the words of John the Baptist are never far behind: "bear fruits worthy of repentance" (Matt 3:8; Luke 3:8). Or, in the words of the apostle Paul, "live your life in a manner worthy of the gospel of Christ" (Phil 1:27). As we saw in chapter 2, God turns human ideas of fasting on their head, calling for a "fast" in the form of sharing your bread with the hungry (Isa 58). God cares deeply what we do in these bodies of ours; in fact, he demands good works from both Christians and non-Christians alike.

Yet problems lurk in deeds we call good. Isaiah's word from the Lord about false and true fasting clues us into the trouble. For all the blatant evil that humans do to flaunt God's commands, no one can deny that humans are religious and moral creatures; we are in fact addicted to religious behaviors and moral judgments. It turns out, however, that these things are just as deadly—if not more so—than outright disobedience. Our good deeds can go sideways in three ways. First, in our excitement for religious, spiritual, or moral actions that appeal to us, we can neglect what God really cares about—just as the Israelites in Isaiah's day performed their ritual fasts but neglected the poor among them. Second, we can do genuinely good deeds for the wrong reason. Third, we can place our trust in our good deeds, essentially making ourselves our own god. All these types of toxic piety can shipwreck our faith even as we appear on the outside to be devoted believers.

The Wrong Deeds

We often think of the sin of Adam and Eve in the Garden as some heinous, blasphemous act. True, they disobeyed a direct command of God—do not eat of the Tree of the Knowledge of Good and Evil. But the name of this tree is no incidental detail. The first sin was not the humans' attempt to create a lawless free-for-all but to take morality into their own hands. They ate because the serpent convinced them that in doing so, they would "know good and evil." We should understand this not as humans crossing some threshold from naiveté to knowledge but as setting themselves up as the ones who "decide good and evil." The fundamental human sin is motivated by the desire to be ethicists.[2] God is quite aware of this basic problem, which is why he told the Israelites, "you shall not do...whatever is right in [your] own eyes," rather do what God commands (Deut 12:8, 32 ESV).[3] Yet sinful humans continue to select the piety that suits them. Such self-chosen works come in two forms.

Well-Meaning Wrong Deeds

Some self-selected religious works are seemingly innocent, or at least well-intentioned. An example of this is the ritual handwashing that the Pharisees criticized Jesus and his disciples for neglecting. Of course, washing one's hands as a religious practice is not bad or sinful *in itself*. And the Pharisees may have had good reasons for the practice: As described above, such practices could bond and strengthen a minority and endangered group. But because God did not command it, we also cannot say that it is righteous in itself. As Jesus sees it, this practice was toxic piety for the Pharisees because it had become

[2] See Timothy J. Wengert, *The Augsburg Confession: Renewing Lutheran Faith and Practice* (Minneapolis: Fortress, 2020), 34–35.

[3] LW 44:46.

a smokescreen. They "clean the outside of the dish, but inside [they] are full of greed and wickedness" (Luke 11:39). Putting their religious efforts into making themselves *appear* good (To themselves? To others? To God?), they neglected what God really cares about.

Consider ways your own piety priorities can get out of whack. You may give a lot to your church, which on the surface is a good thing. But sometimes the same people who are generous at the offering plate are the ones who steamroll others in decisions about how to spend the money. Maybe you are a dedicated volunteer at your local food bank, serving almost as many hours as the employees. But it's possible these hours spent doing "good" mean you rarely see your family. Even when our pious practices seem harmless, they aid sin when they provide an excuse to overlook God's commandments.

Spiritual Wrong Deeds

Other self-selected works are just bad ideas, period. We can't lay down a universal rule for deeds to avoid (beyond whatever clearly opposes God's commandments), but the most worrisome works that are nonetheless attractive to many believers are those that stress the "spiritual" at the expense of the "material." This includes any practice whose motivation is a search for emotional or ecstatic experience or that treats the stuff of creation as something harmful to be avoided as much as possible. The history of Christian monasticism unfortunately provides many extreme examples of such self-chosen piety. In the heyday of so-called desert monasticism, for instance, some monks were famous for living for decades at the top of pillars, constantly exposed to the elements, so they could pursue their austere spirituality with little interference from the world. They literally tried to get closer to heaven and further from the world. (Not coincidentally, the first of these pillar monks, Simeon, earned his renown for purportedly surviving an extreme Lenten fast, going without food or water for the entire forty days.[4]) According to the apostle Paul, practices that seem the most "spiritual" are actually the most blatant signs of a "human way of thinking." Writing to the Colossians (2:16-23), Paul warned against "self-abasement and worship of angels," especially when those insisting on such practices were themselves "dwelling on visions." If you submit to rules against using and enjoying the things of creation ("Do not handle, Do not taste, Do not touch"), this does not mean you are pursuing some advanced spirituality but rather losing your life-giving connection to Christ. When I was a young evangelical, I briefly committed to listening to only Christian music, convinced that enjoying non-Christian music was sinful, or at least showed that you were not as holy or faithful as you could be. I'll admit, this is not the most severe practice. But the notion behind it was that I should be spending my time focusing on things "of God" rather than "of the world." The logic of such behavior is appealing—shouldn't we strive for spiritual things by forsaking material things? But in reality, as the apostle Paul argues, such "self-imposed piety, humility, and severe treatment of the body" only cuts us off from true spiritual nourishment.

[4] I hasten to add that monasticism should not be summarily judged by these excesses. Furthermore, the intent to escape worldly affairs is complicated by the fact that the fame of many of these ascetics attracted needy persons of all kinds. These monks ironically procured a power to intervene in worldly affairs by virtue of their renunciation of the world. Robert Doran, trans., *The Lives of Simeon Stylites* (Kalamazoo, MI: Cistercian, 1992).

This does not mean, though, that God withholds all comforting, thrilling, or blissful spiritual experiences, even visions that seem to take us out of this world. But these encounters come with two important qualifications. First, God gives these completely at his discretion, not in response to our striving after them. As a Pentecostal believer in my teenage years, I remember "tarrying" (a kind of fervent waiting) for emotional touches of the Holy Spirit that went by names like a "fresh outpouring" or an "anointing." Often, those who waited and hoped for remarkable experiences got them, perhaps even showing them with bodily tremors, speaking in tongues, or being "slain in the Spirit" (falling in a trance-like state). But one cannot say for certain that these experiences are the work of the Holy Spirit when social pressures and emotional contagion are just as likely explanations.

Second, these extraordinary spiritual experiences bring great danger. In 2 Corinthians 12:1-10, Paul relates his own remarkable experience of being "caught up to the third heaven." In this supernatural taste of "Paradise" he heard and saw things "that no mortal is permitted to repeat." Mystics of many stripes throughout history have hungered for just such an experience. In some Christian circles, I've heard so-called prayer warriors report that they became so caught up in the spiritual joys of prayer that several hours would go by without their noticing. But Paul immediately notes a potential problem. This experience could make him conceited, lifting him so far off the ground (so to speak) that he forgets that he is dust enlivened by God's Spirit (see chapter 1). As some in those same circles who praised the prayer warrior occasionally said, it's possible for someone to become too heavenly minded to be any earthly good. To prevent this, Paul testifies, God imposed a "thorn" in his flesh through a messenger of Satan. Back in chapter 3 we explored briefly how this incident stymies neat distinctions between God's work and the devil's. But here we notice that in this "torment," Paul heard God teaching him a lesson: "My grace is sufficient for you, for power is made perfect in weakness." If our "spiritual" strength is Christ himself, it will not show up in anything we call our own, including any remarkable spiritual experience. Furthermore, this strength will be of the same upside-down type as Christ's—a power made perfect in weakness, glory displayed through death on the cross.

Other People Imposing Wrong Deeds on Us

In the cases of both the human-chosen works that are not problematic in themselves and those that are plainly ill-conceived, we must beware especially of how others might impose demands on us. Toxic piety often emerges in situations where spiritual leaders insist on strict adherence to human-fashioned rules. (By the way, today, these "spiritual leaders" are just as likely to be politicians, celebrity academics, social-media influencers, and corporate spokespersons as traditional religious figures.) Not only does this unnecessarily constrict peoples' lives, but it harms their consciences.

Many years ago, I decided to join my middle school baseball team. A couple of weeks into practices, I started to get a sick feeling in my stomach. My pastors told me frequently that I must pray, and wait to hear God's answer, before I made any big decision. That sick feeling was being "convicted," as we would say, because I had not given God an opportunity to have his say about this decision. I was already quite a busy young man, with church and work commitments that made it difficult for me to give much effort or attention to baseball.

But rather than simply admitting that I had bit off more than I could chew, I wrestled with the feeling of having sinned—even though a middle schooler playing baseball without hearing God's voice in the matter is no sin.

Perhaps the deeper problem of human-fashioned piety that others impose on us is that it never works. This overlaps with toxic piety of the "wrong trust" kind that I'll explore below, but it is especially easy to see when we give in to others' demands or suggestions for pious practices that God has not commanded. Paul also dealt with this in his blunt assessment of the Colossians' spiritual problems, urging believers to defy those who require certain practices and dole out judgments based on how well people submitted to their peculiar code of conduct (2:16-18). Of course, unless we belong to one of the most intense fundamentalist communities, we are not likely to experience the heavy-handed pressures the Colossians faced. More subtly, today's spiritual elites try to convince us to do things that God does not command by selling them to us as routes to peace, self-care, and assurance, which is another way of saying that they are cures for stress, anxiety, and doubt. Some of the more common suggestions in our day are gratitude journals, mediation, and mindfulness practices (a close spiritual cousin to meditation). And although such practices may have good effects, they don't address the root of the infection—a bad conscience. As I explored in chapter 1 ("Dust"), our sinfulness triggers God's wrath, and we sense God's wrath in feelings of insecurity, fear, and guilt. Whether we acknowledge it or not, our search for wholeness by submitting to human wellness programs is an attempt to satisfy God's wrath. But the math never adds up, for how can one ever know he's done enough to cancel his sins or convince God to drop the charges?[5] What you think is freeing you is really enslaving you, keeping you spinning on a spiritual hamster wheel.

We are hardwired to do works that seem good to us and to others. Yet from God's perspective many of these practices are just plain wrong. We may be doing things God never commanded and that distract us from what he really wants. We may be pursuing our own ideas of what is spiritual but, in the process, only demonstrating that we have lost confidence that in Christ, we have all the Spirit we need. Compounding and often fueling these problems, we may submit to other people's misguided or misleading ideas of what we should do. Sadly, though, these are not the only types of toxic piety that plague us.

The Wrong Reasons

Another type of toxic piety is less obvious because it hides in works that God has declared good. In the Gospel reading that begins Lent for many, Jesus criticizes those he calls "hypocrites" for the way they give to the poor, pray, and fast. Fasting is not a general commandment from God (see chapter 2), but God does command giving to the poor and prayer, while leaving open the specifics on these practices (for example, Deut 15:11; Ps 50:15). Regardless, all these behaviors are righteous on their face. Jews of Jesus' day often invoked this triplet of

[5] This is a paraphrase of *Apology of the Augsburg Confession*, art. 20: "If the forgiveness of sins were given on account of our works, when would we know that we had taken hold of it, when would a terrified conscience find a work it could consider sufficient to conciliate the wrath of God?" Robert Kolb and Timothy J. Wengert, eds., *The Book of Concord: The Confessions of the Evangelical Lutheran Church* (Minneapolis: Fortress, 2000), 236. As the Augsburg Confession (art. 20) states, "This whole teaching [of good works] must be referred to that struggle of the terrified conscience, and it cannot be understood apart from that struggle." Kolb and Wengert, 55.

good deeds as shorthand for being a good person. In the same book of Tobit mentioned above, we find this basic summary of Jewish piety:

> Do good, and evil will not overtake you. Prayer with fasting is good, but better than both is almsgiving with righteousness. (Tobit 12:7-8)

Jesus, however, is not so sure that prayer, fasting, and almsgiving are always good. From God's perspective, the same deeds may be righteousness or hypocrisy. The key distinction is the *reason* for doing the deed. As Jesus says, "Beware of practicing your piety before others in order to be seen by them; for then you have no reward from your Father in heaven" (Matt 6:1). When we perform our good deeds in order to display our goodness to others, these deeds will not be good in God's eyes.

Today, we have a label for this type of behavior, although it may not often entail things like fasting. We call it "virtue signaling."[6] Communicating our virtuous qualities to others may be essential to human survival, as some scientists claim.[7] But American culture currently suffers a virtue signaling epidemic that some describe as "moralitis."[8] Humans are naturally prone to Us-and-Them thinking, where Us is held together by, among other things, a common moral code.[9] This becomes hard to maintain, however, in a pluralistic soci-

---

[6] James Bartholomew, "The Awful Rise of 'Virtue Signalling,'" *The Spectator*, April 18, 2015. Bartholomew claims to have coined the term.

[7] Geoffrey Miller, *Virtue Signaling: Essays on Darwinian Politics & Free Speech* (n.p.: Cambrian Moon, 2019).

[8] Robert Oulds and Niall McCrae, *Moralitis, A Cultural Virus* (London: The Bruges Group, 2020).

[9] Joshua Greene, *Moral Tribes: Emotion, Reason, and the Gap Between Us and Them* (New York: Penguin, 2013).

ety where we frequently interact with those who do not share our moral code. This leads to the inclination to advertise our own moral commitments and condemn others'—behavior that is greased by social media platforms that work much better for declaring opinions than engaging in conversation.

Examples of this are not hard to find. Some are high-profile. University administrators routinely issue public "statements" staking moral claims on hot-button issues of the day: policing, Black Lives Matter, the Supreme Court decision on abortion, and violence in Ukraine and the Middle East.[10] In the midst of the Covid-19 pandemic, leading scientists signaled their opposition to anti-Asian sentiment by publicly rejecting the so-called lab leak theory of the virus' origins, well before the evidence supported such a sweeping disavowal.[11] This phenomenon is so common that you may wonder if the toys parents buy for their child are "moral theater"—perhaps they're signaling their social views through the races of their child's dolls or the disregard for traditional gender roles associated with their toys.[12] I've

---

[10] Blake Smith, "Opinion | Do Administrators Think They're Spiritual Healers?," The Chronicle of Higher Education, October 12, 2022, https://www.chronicle.com/article/do-administrators-think-theyre-spiritual-healers.

[11] For the scientists' statement, see, Charles Calisher et al., "Statement in Support of the Scientists, Public Health Professionals, and Medical Professionals of China Combatting COVID-19," *The Lancet* 395, no. 10226 (March 7, 2020): e42–43, https://doi.org/10.1016/S0140-6736(20)30418-9. In addition to the virtue-signal value, this statement seems to have been motivated also by business interests. Eric Winsberg, "Opinion | We Need Scientific Dissidents Now More Than Ever," The Chronicle of Higher Education, August 10, 2023, https://www.chronicle.com/article/we-need-scientific-dissidents-now-more-than-ever.

[12] Tyler Austin Harper, "Opinion | The Moral Theater of Social Justice Parenting," *The New York Times*, September 24, 2023, sec. Opinion, https://www.nytimes.com/2023/09/24/opinion/social-justice-parenting.html.

noticed a growing trend of men at parks, malls, and restaurants wearing t-shirts with quippy messages relating to being a dad. I may be getting cynical and overthinking things, but I sense that on some level, such apparel is signaling virtue. Through the allusions to Star Wars or Jurassic Park, the shirts are basically saying, "I am a father who is caring and invested in my children." Virtue signaling comes from both those who are expressing genuine values and those who are complete frauds. The common denominator is that they perform some perceived righteous act to be seen by others. The *reason* for the act is to craft a righteous public image of oneself; the *signal* is the important thing, not the deed itself.

Because morality infuses politics in our culture, we must note that people of all political persuasions engage in virtue signaling. And they often use Christian terms and symbols. In the weeks and months after the tragedy of 9/11, nearly every city block in the United States had at least one business with a message like "God Loves America" on its marquee. More recently, we witness political candidates campaigning on slogans like "Jesus, Guns, Babies." And we see memes in our social media feed lamenting that Jesus would today be condemned as a "socialist" for his efforts to heal the sick and cure the lame. Whatever the merits of these views and any behaviors connected with them, Jesus condemns the hypocrisy of those whose main concern is crafting their righteous persona for others to see. As Jesus suggests, the best "reward" one can receive for such behavior is the attention and possibly the admiration of other people (aka social media "likes"); but such admiration will not count a lick on judgment day.

The Wrong Trust

The piety of virtue signaling is toxic because people do it to show off to others. But the correction is not as simple as changing the audience from humans to God. Although Jesus advised us to perform our piety "in secret" where God alone sees, another danger hides in the way we relate to our good works when we stand before God. In short, this final type of toxic piety occurs when we put our trust in our good works for our status before God. Luke's Gospel gives us two memorable parables for understanding this hazard. In both parables, Jesus contrasts two men—one who has lived by the rules and another who should not be a role model for anyone.

> Read Luke 18:9-14, and write your responses to these questions:
>
> 1. What are the obvious sins that you are grateful you have not fallen prey to? Has someone close to you been guilty of these?
> 2. What are the signs that a person feels sorrow for sin?
> 3. Recall a time in your life when you felt extremely unworthy of God's love. What led to that point? What brought you out of it?
> 4. What does it mean to be "justified"?

In the "Parable of the Pharisee and the Tax Collector," the Pharisee thanks God that he has not committed obvious sins like theft and adultery. To put a fine point on his prayer, he even thanks God that he is not like the tax collector who prays near him. Instead, he reminds God, "I fast twice a week; I give a tenth of all my income" (18:12). Here we have a return of two parts of the triplet of first-century Jewish piety. For his part, the tax-collector prays, too. But his prayer could not be more different; instead of thanking God for his righteousness and reminding God of his good deeds, he simply prays for mercy. As Jesus explains, the one who is justified after his prayer is not the one with a resumé of righteousness but the one who knows his sins and seeks God's unmerited favor. The Pharisee's error was to trust his righteousness rather than God's mercy. No amount of personal piety is enough to justify you in God's eyes.

The long parable in Luke 15 most often goes by the title "The Parable of the Prodigal Son." But the message of Jesus' parable would be better conveyed by calling it "The Parable of the Obedient Son and the Wayward Son." Again, the point is the contrast between one man with a spotless record and another who is a moral mess. As the familiar story goes, the "prodigal" son, the one who insulted his father by demanding his inheritance and wasted it in sinful pursuits, came to his senses and returned home, humbly seeking any scrap of pity from his father. Most interpretations of the story put great stress on the mercy of the father to receive his wayward son back into his home and even celebrate the son's return with a lavish feast. Just as important, however, is the way the story ends for the other son. Like the Pharisee in the other parable touting his good deeds to God, this elder son reminds his father, "I have never disobeyed your command" (15:29). The father, however, will not play the elder son's game of measuring the father's favor by the son's righteous deeds.

So, the son who did everything right is the one left out of the party, because he trusted his own obedience rather than his father's grace.

Because this toxic piety is not about the deeds themselves but rather the trust in the deeds, this danger can accompany any practices one might imagine are pleasing to God—whether God has commanded them or we choose them for ourselves. And because the problem is an unseen matter of the heart, it can be hard to diagnose. What is particularly unnerving is that this toxicity damages regular, well-meaning Christians. You don't need to be seeking special spiritual experiences or puffing up your image in the eyes of others to be at risk of this danger. The fatal flaw lodges itself in the elder son's earnest obedience to his father and the Pharisee's steadfast charity. Likewise, in our own day, it is lodged in the faithful churchgoing, generous philanthropy, committed volunteering, dutiful prayer, Bible study, and devotional practices (maybe even reading this book!) of everyday believers.

Of course, these things are not bad, but we can use them wrongly. Like the Pharisee and elder son, we use them as bargaining chips or self-defense. The problem creeps into all the moments where we imagine what God thinks of us. When you need or want something desperately from God, you entertain a notion that God *should* give you what you ask for, since you give regularly to the church. When you try to reason through your suffering, you feel confident that God is not causing your pain, since you haven't done anything to deserve it. In severe moments (such as in the wake of a loved one's death) when you contemplate your end and the judgment to follow, you offer yourself the comfort that you can't possibly have a bad outcome, since there are so many other worse sinners. In each case, you look for assurance that God will view you favorably because of your good deeds or your refraining from evil.

This would seem to put us in a bind. As we will explore in the next section, believers literally cannot *not* do good. Yet the awareness of our own good deeds is the seed of a deadly temptation. In Jesus' warnings about toxic piety in Matthew 6, he tells us that when we give (not *if*), we should not let our left hand know what the right hand is doing (v3). In other words, we are most blessed in our good deeds when we are unaware of them. This may sound less like a solution and more like an acknowledgment of the believer's Catch-22. At the very least, the next time someone tries to pat you on the back for your kindness or generosity, your immediate reaction should be, "How dare you threaten my salvation by accusing me of a good deed. Take it back!" We believers must be ever vigilant against the tendency to put our trust in what we do rather than in what God does for us.

Clearly, our attempts at performing good deeds can go wrong in many ways. We focus on our own ideas of what is good at the expense of what God really wants. Even when we do what God has commanded, we show off for others or we fool ourselves into thinking these deeds make us good in God's eyes. Toxic piety abounds. But the situation is not hopeless. In the next section, we'll see how God gives us clear guidance and ample opportunities to do real good deeds.

True Good Works

With all the spiritual dangers that come with piety, we might wonder if it's worth the risk. But unfortunately, we can't opt out. We live in bodies (including our minds) that *must* serve either sin or righteousness. As Bob Dylan memorably sang in his gospel phase, "you're gonna have to serve somebody," either Satan or God. In Paul's words to his fellow believers, "For just as you once presented your members as slaves to impurity and to greater and greater iniquity, so now present your members as slaves to righteousness for sanctification" (Rom 6:19). There is no third way. Wise believers, then, ask two questions: First, *what good works should we do*? Second, *how do we do them?*

Our discussion of true good works calls for a careful distinction at the outset. God requires certain works from everybody. God lays out clear *oughts* and *shoulds* for all humanity. When we are obedient to these requirements, other people will often reward our deeds (or at least, by obeying the rules, we will avoid punishment). But these good deeds do not, on their own, count as righteousness before God—this is the trap of the "wrong trust" toxic piety.

The works that God requires of all humans show up in many places. All human cultures have a basic code of conduct: Don't take what isn't yours; don't harm people who pose no immediate threat to you or your neighbors. You can find these scattered in religious texts, governmental legislation, and on the walls of kindergarten classrooms. These requirements are not merely the "product" of culture, they are inscribed on human hearts, so that we can talk about a "conscience" that all people have (Rom 2:15). We who look to the Bible are fortunate to have this code inscribed as the Ten Commandments. Moses delivered plainly in a neat package what exists in more scattered ways in other cultures. These commandments are not for Jews and Christians only, but this is our starting point for good works. God really does want husbands and wives to be faithful to one another, children to honor their parents, and people to tell the truth about each other. Whether these commandments are in the form of "thou shalt" or "thou shalt not," each commandment prohibits certain behavior *and* urges certain behavior. God's intention for marriage is not just about refraining from adultery. God also insists that husbands and wives love, respect, and honor each other in all things. God's intent for human property is not simply that people would not steal. God also requires that neighbors help each other protect their property and flourish in using it.[13]

For those who expect Christianity to have particularly piercing insight on ethical issues, and for those who come to the faith as adults, this can be a letdown. The initial answer to how a Christian ought to live is the same as the answer to how an unbeliever ought to live. In most of life, no one should be able to tell the difference between a virtuous Christian and a virtuous non-Christian.[14] This is true not only because the same commandments apply to both, but because God calls both Christians and non-Christians to the same walks of life, or *vocations*.[15] The jobs and relationships God calls us to is the rubber that meets the road of the Ten Commandments. We examine our own obedience to the commandments in light of the particular temptations and opportunities of our vocations. Has the father provided for

[13] Martin Luther summarizes the dual nature of the commandments in *Small Catechism*, Kolb and Wengert, *Book of Concord*, 351–54.

[14] Jonathan Malesic, *Secret Faith in the Public Square: An Argument for the Concealment of Christian Identity* (Grand Rapids, MI: Brazos, 2009). Malesic argues that keeping Christian identity hidden in the public square mitigates the problems of self-righteousness and the corruption of faith that occurs when believers use their Christian identity to secure advantages in the world.

[15] Christopher J. Richmann, *Called: Recovering Lutheran Principles for Ministry and Vocation* (Minneapolis: Fortress, 2022). One vocation, namely minister of the gospel, inherently signifies Christian associations.

and appropriately disciplined his children? Has the businessman been honest in all his transactions? Has the employer sought the welfare of her employees rather than seeking only to maximize profits?

This workaday righteousness is the thrust of the so-called household codes of the New Testament. These are passages where the writer gives direction for how people within the same household should regard each other and treat each other (in the ancient world, "household" included servants as well as family relations). See, for instance, Colossians 3:18-24. Wives respect husbands. Husbands love wives. Children obey parents. Fathers deal evenhandedly with their children. Workers do what their boss asks. Nothing distinctly Christian or particularly spiritual about any of it. This ordinary quality is part of the genius of piety rooted in the commandments and vocations, from a spiritual perspective. It's hard for your ego to get inflated over being honest in business or bringing home a paycheck so your children can eat. In Paul's language, there is little risk of becoming conceited about one's own righteousness. Yet Christians have, in faith, the added assurance that such mundane good works are part of God's grand plan for our lives. As Paul says, "For we are what he has made us, created in Christ Jesus for good works, which God prepared beforehand to be *our walk of life*" (Eph 2:10). In our daily tasks as spouse, employee, citizen, and sibling, we simply walk forward—one foot in front of the other—into the good works God has set out for us. In most cases, this does not require great ethical calculation or spiritual discernment, much less "listening" for God's voice. God's will is clear at the intersection of the Ten Commandments and our particular vocations; in this space, God (or rather, God, through our neighbors) wrings good works from us like water from a sponge.[16] This is why, for another congregation, Paul urged believers, "let each of you lead the life that the Lord has assigned, to which God called you" (1 Cor 7:17). Paul is encouraging Christians to live out their faith by committing themselves to whatever roles they find themselves in—parents, workers, friends. You don't need to mount a forty-foot pillar to get closer to God, for whatever life God has assigned you, "there [you] remain with God" (1 Cor 7:24).

This may sound like there is nothing special about Christian piety. But in fact, God expects Christians to practice one habit that you will not often see among non-believers. This habit is *giving up what you think you deserve in order to care for another.* This comes in many forms: offering a second cheek to someone who has already hit you (Matt 5:39); looking to the interests of others before your own (Phil 2:4); repaying evil with good (Rom 12:17-21); humbly serving those who by worldly reasoning rank lower than you (John 13); forgiving hundreds of times the same sinner committing the same sin against you over and again (Matt 18:21-22). In any of these cases, God calls Christians not to do what is fair or justified; rather, God calls Christians to sacrifice what they have a perfectly good right to—safety, retribution, equity. Of course, believers don't do this to receive praise as heroes or martyrs but genuinely to serve others and bring glory to God (Matt 5:16).

An example from Scripture illustrates how this works. For many early Christians, the stunning beauty of the gospel was that one was

[16] As the Augsburg Confession (art. 20) states, Evangelical (in this case, Lutheran) "writings on the Decalogue [that is, the Ten Commandments]...bear witness and have given instruction concerning all kinds and walks of life; what manner of life and which activities in every calling please God. Kolb and Wengert, *Book of Concord*, 53.

free from traditional religious dietary restrictions. Someone who before becoming a Christian had lived her entire life avoiding certain foods and drinks celebrated freedom in Christ with every bite of meat or sip of wine. But these "strong" believers lived alongside those of "weak" faith. For the weak believers, witnessing or feeling pressure to exercise this freedom would be highly offensive or cause them to go against their own consciences. Addressing this situation, Paul advised the "strong faith" crowd to "not let what you eat cause the ruin of one for whom Christ died" (Rom 14:15). One can easily see how this situation could have devolved into bitterness and chaos—the "strong" digging in their heels on a principled stand for gospel freedom, virtue signaling with T-shirts screen-printed with images of pork and wine while the "weak" write derisive op-eds denouncing this behavior in the name of moral clarity. But in light of the gospel, Christians must put aside their own rights and freedoms (even freedoms *rooted in the gospel*) for the sake of others—especially when exercising such rights might lead a fellow believer to sin.

As we've seen, we are prone to all sorts of problems with our works of piety. But for the most part, true good works are not mysterious or complicated. The Ten Commandments tell us what to do, and our vocations give us opportunities to do them. Beyond this, God calls Christians to the higher standard of putting other's needs ahead of our own entitlements. Furthermore, the Bible teaches us that although we must do these good works, we will never perfectly perform what God requires. And even if we could, God does not save us or consider us righteous because of what we do. For these reasons, we need a clear idea of where good deeds really come from.

The Source of Good Works

Let's not kid ourselves—giving up what you think you deserve isn't easy. Addressing a different situation, Paul posed the rhetorical question that forces us to face reality: "Why not rather be wronged?" (1 Cor 6:7). When you dig deep enough, all people who are *not* willing to be wronged are concerned about establishing their own rightness. If the wrongdoer gets away with it, how can the wronged person feel righteous by comparison? The piety of giving up your rights, then, only works for the long haul if you are certain that your righteousness comes from a different source. This, along with the recognition that no good deeds themselves count as righteousness before God, reframes our usual approach to good works. As important as it is to know what deeds are good, we will be spinning our wheels if we do not know *where good works come from.*

Scripture offers a consistent answer. True good works come from faith. We could explain this in two ways. First, faith is the source of good deeds because only by faith in Christ's death and resurrection for us do we receive what we try—but always fail—to obtain through our own good deed programs: righteousness in God's sight (Gen 15:6; Rom 4). In this sense, faith is the source of good deeds from the human perspective, *psychologically*. When faith frees us from trying to impress God or prove our worth to him with what we do, we can, finally, see our neighbors as the proper objects of our piety. In the topsy-turvy logic of the gospel, this makes our good works truly good in God's sight; they are no longer performed for God's benefit (which he does not need) but for the benefit of God's creation. Faith allows us to do good works as God originally intended, plunging us ever more deeply into our vocations where we meet our neighbor in need.

Psychology on its own, however, does not explain how good deeds spring from faith. We must also describe this *theologically*—that is, from God's perspective. Faith does not happen without the Holy Spirit. This is true in a double way: The Spirit is both the *cause* of faith and the *gift* that accompanies faith. But we should not think of this gift as some power that multiplies our natural abilities, some spiritual turbo boost for our human engines. Recall from chapter 1 that baptism is no mere symbol or ritual; it is dying and rising with Christ. As faith links to baptism, the giving of the Spirit in faith is death and resurrection; it is a new creation. In other words, the Holy Spirit doesn't make an improved you but a *new* you. The prophet Ezekiel describes this combination of baptism-Spirit-gift as a "new heart" (Ezek 36:25-27). By faith, we are risen with Christ, and so we "walk in newness of life" (Rom 6:4). Remade as "good trees," we can't help but bear "good fruit" (Matt 7:17-18). This new creation, living in the Spirit, produces good works with such consistency, and in such ordinary circumstances, that we are liable to overlook them as good deeds at all. And that is kind of the point: Your left hand won't know what your right hand is doing as you simply live righteously in the ebb and flow of ordinary life. This was Martin Luther's great discovery when he defended the teaching on vocation against both Catholics and other Protestants who wanted a more spiritual piety: "Spiritual" does not mean the opposite of material (or bodily); "spiritual" means that which comes from the Holy Spirit.[17]

Still, in the midst of this earthy piety, the Holy Spirit does do something remarkable. We witness in our bodies a piety beyond human abilities, a piety free from God's law but never opposed to God's law:

[17] LW 37:94.

> The fruit of the Spirit is love, joy, peace, patience, kindness, generosity, faithfulness, gentleness, and self-control. There is no law against such things. (Gal 5:22-23)

This is a piety that forgives rather than demanding justice, that gives instead of expecting payment, that does for others without thinking or remembering or even being asked. And the only source of this piety is faith. In fact, faith is so crucial that without it, even the most conscientious behavior is sin (Rom 14:23). But with faith, even picking up a piece of straw is a good work.[18] To return to Daniel and the Pharisees from the opening of this chapter, vegetarianism and handwashing can be good works when one knows that righteousness comes as a free gift apart from works. Faith is, then, in a manner of speaking, the original good work (just as unbelief was the original sin) that makes all other good works possible and encompasses them all. In Luther's words from a small book on good works, faith is "the first, highest, and most precious of all good works," from which all other good works "receive a borrowed goodness."[19] When the worried crowds asked Jesus, "What must we do to perform the works of God?," his answer was simple: "This is the work of God, that you believe in him whom he has sent" (John 6:28-29).

You do not need to be worried that you are not doing the right thing or doing enough good. In the first place, God has given us ample direction and opportunity for good works through the commandments and our vocations. But even more important, faith itself is a gift from God, and faith *will* bring forth good works, whether

---

[18] LW 44:25.

[19] LW 44:23.

you are aware of them or not. And that is the grand theme of Lent and the entire Christian life. God is in control, inflicting your death and raising you to new life, imposing fasts on you, testing you to exercise and strengthen your faith, giving you the gift of repentance, and producing good works out of repentance. In all these ways, like the stretching of daylight in Spring, God stretches you on the cross with Christ. As we have seen throughout this study, this can be unsettling, frustrating, painful, and agonizing. But just as it was for the criminal hanging on his own cross next to Jesus (Luke 23:39-43), it is the gateway to paradise.

Concluding Meditation

God demands that we do good deeds, but it's easy to get tripped up along the way. We sinful creatures turn good works toxic by devoting ourselves to faux-spiritual practices God has not commanded, performing our piety to be admired by others, and trusting our deeds to make us good in God's eyes. But true piety must do what God has commanded in the abundant opportunities that arise from the daily work of our many vocations. Above this, believers forsake their own rights for the sake of others. This impossible task is only accomplished by faith in God's favor, which relieves us of trying to be righteous and by the Holy Spirit brings a new creation that does good before it is asked.

QUESTIONS FOR DISCUSSION:

1. In what ways do you "signal" your morality and virtues to others?

2. Which of these pitfalls do you struggle most with: doing the wrong things, doing things for the wrong reasons, or relying too much on your own efforts?

3. List your five most important vocations. What is one temptation to sin and one opportunity for good that accompanies each calling?

4. Name a moment when you have been surprised to learn that you were helpful or appreciated.

Appendix
THE ORIGINS OF LENT

When thinking about the days or times that are most important to Christians, Lent may not be the first thing that comes to mind. Today, in cultures that have historical Christian roots, the marquee holiday—and holy season—is Christmas. Societies that have long ago abandoned their overt Christian elements still close offices, businesses, and most governmental services for the day that honors the birth of Jesus Christ. Public schools shut down for at least a week around the holiday, Christmas music begins playing on secular radio stations two months before the big day, and festive decorations make their appearance in retail stores a month earlier than that (and my neighbor adorns his yard with Christmas decorations the day after Halloween!). Every year, Santa Claus, mistletoe, carols, and eggnog punctuate "the most wonderful time of the year." But historically, Easter—not Christmas—is the religious holiday that sets the terms for the entire year.

Two factors help explain why this is so. First, Scripture gives us precise details about the day and time of Jesus' resurrection, a courtesy it does not extend to Jesus' birth.[1] Second, the *event* of Jesus'

---

[1] Luke 2:1-2 states that Jesus was born during the reign of Ceasar Augustus while Quirinius was governor of Syria. But this provides no help determining the appropriate date for a recurring celebration.

resurrection—along with his death, for he could not rise without first having died—bears greater theological significance than the event of Jesus' birth. Of course, the *fact* of Jesus' birth matters greatly, but as I preach frequently to my congregation around Christmas time, the incarnation does not save anybody.[2]

Rather than Jesus' birth, his resurrection is the event that anchors the classic Christian sense of time.[3] The earliest Christians celebrated Christ's resurrection with modest weekly worship on Sundays, often before dawn. As the Gospels maintain that Jesus rose from the dead early on the first day of the week, Christians gathered each first day to commemorate and proclaim the resurrection, often poetically referring to Sunday as the "eighth day," since Christ's resurrection brings a new creation in faith outside the bounds of the original seven-day weekly cycle.

Christ's resurrection was the culmination of events in Jesus' last few days. So the logic that placed weekly worship on Sunday led to seeing each week as a reprise of holy week. For this reason, many early Christians fasted every Friday in honor of Jesus' crucifixion and Wednesday in remembrance of Judas' conspiracy to betray Jesus. I list the days in this order (rather than chronologically, Wednesday-Friday) to stress that Easter is the point of departure; other observances get their meaning from Christ's resurrection, in a sort of

---

[2] It was necessary for the Son of God to be born of a woman and born under the law (Gal 4:4), but only in Jesus' death does God deal with our sins, and only in his resurrection does God make us righteous (Rom 4:25).

[3] The following synopsis of the history of Lent is informed by Adolf Adam, *The Liturgical Year: Its History and Its Meaning after the Reform of the Liturgy*, trans. Matthew J. O'Connell (Collegeville, MN: Liturgical Press, 1990); Thomas J. Talley, *The Origins of the Liturgical Year*, 2nd ed. (Collegeville, MN: Liturgical Press, 1991).

reverse-engineering fashion. Imagine Easter as a pebble tossed in a pond, and these other important early observances are the ripples expanding on the surface of the water.

Lent, however, is not a weekly observance but is part of what we call the liturgical year, or simply the church year. In fact, we call it "Lent" because this echoes an old Germanic word for Spring—a word that is related to the English word "lengthen." During Spring, the days lengthen, or stretch, as the hours of daylight steadily increase. But even as a yearly liturgical event, Christ's resurrection is again the anchor for other observances. The Gospels carefully depict Jesus' crucifixion in close connection with the annual Jewish holiday of Passover and precisely date his resurrection to the third day after his death. All early Christians saw the theological significance: Christ became, in the words of the apostle Paul, "our Passover lamb" (1 Cor 5:7 ESV). Since many of the first Christians were Jews who continued observing Jewish holidays (infused with Christian meaning), they also had a fitting annual occurrence for commemorating Jesus' resurrection. This did not mean, however, that all Christians agreed on the precise timing of this yearly festival. Some stuck closer to Jewish roots by celebrating the resurrection on the third day after the Jewish Passover, regardless of the day of the week this landed on (in other words, Easter could fall on any day of the week). Others regarded Sunday as the only proper day for commemorating the resurrection. This disagreement in practice became a surprisingly spirited controversy. And even after the triumph of Sunday as the only appropriate day of the week for Easter, calendar discrepancies remained among various communities.

The dating of Easter had implications for the rest of the liturgical year, again showing the Easter ripple effect. Tracing the biblical narrative, Pentecost fell fifty days after Easter. Even what we now think of as Christmas gets its dating by Easter's radiating power. By some calculations, the Passover of Jesus' death fell on March 25. According to an ancient theory that extraordinary humans died on the same calendar day as their conception (indicating a sort of perfect, complete life), Mary conceived Jesus on this date. Adding nine months for the traditional length of pregnancy put Jesus' birth on December 25. Because Christians east of the Mediterranean used a different calendar, these days fell on April 6 for Mary's conception of Jesus and January 6 for Jesus' birth. Through a messy process of co-mingling these different calendars, the day of Epiphany (which originally celebrated many scenes of Jesus being revealed, including his birth, his baptism, and his first miracle) now falls on January 6 for those who trace their Christian history through the Catholic Church. This also explains why we have "twelve days of Christmas"—the time from Christmas on December 25 to Epiphany on January 6.

Regardless of how Christians calculated the date for Easter or what calendar they used, many believers fasted on the Friday and Saturday before Resurrection Day. This was perhaps an imitation of (or simply continued) the Jewish fast that preceded eating the Passover meal. The mood of this fast was marked by grief, invoking Jesus' words that although his disciples ate freely while he was with them, a time would come when the bridegroom would be taken from them, and they would then fast (Luke 5:35). By the third century, this fast in some places lasted the full week leading to Easter. For some churches, this pre-Easter fast was part of the practice of baptizing on Easter. The church required the ones to be baptized to fast in preparation for their great initiation into the faith, and often, other Christians fasted in solidarity with these converts.

Not until the fourth century did Christians start describing the pre-Easter fast as "forty days." But as precise as this number sounds, it masks a bewildering variety in practice. Some designated eight weeks as the period of fasting to reach this forty-day mark, since they did not fast on Saturdays or Sundays.[4] (By the way, these fasts did not mean completely going without food and water but refraining from eating until supper.) Others were content with six weeks of fasting, which, with Sundays omitted, amounted to 36 fast days—cleverly referred to by many as a "tithe of the year" (36 being approximately one-tenth of the year's days). In some places, the forty days of fasting actually began right after Epiphany. Although also a preparation for baptism, this fast was primarily an imitation of Jesus' experience: Recall that Epiphany was, in part, a commemoration of Jesus' baptism, after which, according to the Gospels, he fasted in the wilderness. For many years, these "forty-day" fasts were separate from the fasts of the week before Easter, with at least two days of feasting between the periods of fasting. In time, the "forty days" came to include the week before Easter and to be taken more literally, numerically speaking. By starting on the Wednesday of the seventh week before Easter Sunday, the faithful could observe exactly forty days of fasting while continuing to omit Sundays. This is the origin

[4] As a rule, Christians did not fast on Sundays, since fasting was a somber practice, and Sunday, as the day of resurrection, was a day for celebrating. Christians in the eastern portions of the Roman empire also did not fast on Saturdays, thus continuing the Jewish tradition of not fasting on the Sabbath.

of what almost all Christians today regard as the beginning of Lent: Ash Wednesday.

This historical tour shows why the springtime fast began on a *Wednesday* forty-six days before Easter, but it does not explain why we call this day *Ash* Wednesday. In a somewhat separate development, the church came to regard the annual commemoration of Jesus' death and resurrection as an appropriate time to welcome back those whom it had banned because of serious sins. This mirrors the practice of baptism on Easter: If this is a fitting occasion for consummating the conversion process, it seems equally appropriate as a time to ratify a re-conversion. In fact, such repentant sinners would be officially "reconciled" on the Thursday before Easter—the day we call Holy Thursday or Maundy Thursday—allowing them to participate in the services commemorating Jesus' last supper, betrayal, crucifixion, and resurrection. Although applying ashes to one's body or face had been a common sign of repentance since Old Testament times (see chapter 4, "Turn"), not until 960 does this practice clearly show up in the historical record in connection with the Wednesday beginning Lent. And only when a pope decreed so in 1091 did this become a general practice of repentance for all believers. By that time, and largely as a result of the Scriptures that were commonly used in worship during the season, all the elements of Lent as we know it were in place—a time of preparation for Easter marked by remembrance of death, self-denial and pious works accompanied by awareness of temptation, and repentance.